LIVING LIFE
THE ESSEX WAY

LIVING LIFE
THE ESSEX WAY
TOWIE & Me

Sam Faiers

**SIMON &
SCHUSTER**

London · New York · Sydney · Toronto · New Delhi

A CBS COMPANY

Thanks to my family and friends, who have
supported me so much, especially Billie and Dad.
But in particular to you, Mum –
this one's for you!

First published in Great Britain by Simon & Schuster UK Ltd, 2012
A CBS COMPANY

Picture credits: 17, 21–3 © PA; 19 © Xposure Photos; 20 © Matrix Pictures

The right of Sam Faiers to be identified as author of this work
has been asserted by her in accordance with sections 77 and 78
of the Copyright, Designs and Patents Act, 1988.

Simon & Schuster UK Ltd
1st Floor
222 Gray's Inn Road
London
WC1X 8HB

www.simonandschuster.co.uk

Simon & Schuster Australia, Sydney
Simon & Schuster India, New Delhi

A CIP catalogue record for this book is available
from the British Library

ISBN: 978-1-84983-978-5

Typeset by M Rules
Printed and bound by CPI Group (UK) Ltd, Croydon, CR0 4YY

CONTENTS

INTRODUCTION

Oxford Dictionary definition of 'Essex girl': noun, British, informal, derogatory: A brash, materialistic young woman of a type supposedly found in Essex or surrounding areas in the southeast of England.

For me, the true definition of 'Essex girl': noun, British, informal, complimentary: A stylish, hard-working, big-hearted and family-minded young woman found in Brentwood or nearby areas (and Marbs).

As Amy Childs came out through the changing room curtain in a wedding dress, I felt a nervous giggle building up in me, and when I tried to speak I couldn't stop grinning. I could sense my friend Harry Derbidge doing the same next to me and was afraid to catch his eye.

I carried on talking, but saw this glint in Amy's eye too, and suddenly I couldn't hold it in, and all three of us got hysterical. We were lying on the floor laughing and couldn't get it together. Hardly likely to be a great TV debut, but then can you blame us? The three of us were filming our first ever scene for *The Only Way Is Essex*, and we were terrified. I was so nervous, but giggling and excited at the same time. We were supposed to just be getting on with our everyday lives, but until you are used to having three cameras filming you, it can hardly be expected to feel very natural, can it? Especially as it was our first time in front of the cameras. We'd only had a rough briefing from the producers, and weren't told how to behave, or even what to expect. So really, we were like three hyperactive kids.

After a stern talking to from the producer, who already had the hump with us, we carried on filming – not that our hysterics were a one-off that first day!

But let's face it, only a few weeks before I had been working in a local bank, plotting how to improve my glamour-modelling career and trying to figure out what to wear to a night out at Sugar Hut that weekend. I hadn't realised that within a couple of months I would be on one of the most discussed TV shows in the UK and written about in newspapers and magazines practically every day – something which has had both good and bad effects on my life, as you'll read about later. I would be able to earn in an hour what I earned in a month at the bank,

I am living my dream right now

and would be having experiences I had never dreamed of, not to mention the chance to open my own shop. It really does feel like I am living my dream right now. And I even get to do it all while still living in the best place in the world – Essex!

This book is my way of giving you a taste of my life growing up, what it is like being on *TOWIE* and what it means to be a true Essex girl. I hope you enjoy it – make sure you give me a tweet @SamanthaFaiers to let me know. And remember: don't be jel, be reem!

Sam faiers x

Sam Faiers

1

HOW THE *TOWIE*
DREAM BEGAN

So I guess you want to know how I got to be on *The Only Way Is Essex* in the first place, because being a show about ordinary people, it's not like you can work towards getting cast. Being from Essex was perhaps the only qualification needed. But it was a more complicated route to the show than just that.

I know people in the public eye say this all the time, but I honestly never imagined that I would be famous one day. Other than when I was a kid, plotting to be in the next Spice Girls or something, I wasn't one of those teenagers who dream of being a celebrity and spend all their time working out how to do it. You would never have seen me in a queue for the *X Factor* auditions!

Weirdly though, if you ask any of my schoolmates who they thought would end up being the famous one, they are all like, 'Oh my God, yeah, blatantly it would be you, Sam!' One of my mates reminded me that at primary school I did cheerleading and became obsessed with the film *Bring It On*. So when I was in Year 6 I insisted we had a cheerleading team too, and I loved being in it and showing off. So maybe wanting to be centre of attention was in me after all …

By the time *TOWIE* came along, I'd already had a taste of TV. I'd been in the *Live & Kicking* studio audience twice, and on *The Sooty Show* once – when they had filmed in Spain, where my family had a house – I was sat on the beach with the puppets! But apart from those Oscar-winning appearances, I'd had no experience of it, and wasn't even thinking about getting on TV. Instead I was focused on getting myself established as a glamour model, and although I knew it wouldn't last forever, it was my aim at the time. I also had a full-time job in a local bank, and hoped to progress there too. I was 18, and my aim was just to earn more so I could have more fun, as well as saving for the future. I had a manager to help with my modelling, but I didn't have a proper agent at this point. Celebrities were just people I read about in magazines in my spare time.

Meanwhile, Brian Belo, who came from Essex, had just won the eighth series of *Big Brother*. After the show finished, he was always at Sugar Hut partying and basically making the most of his new celebrity status, as you would. Because of that he was friends with Kirk Norcross, who owns Sugar Hut, and Amy Childs, as she was always there with Kirk. Then he got to know me through Amy, although he says he had heard about me before that, through other people – all complimentary, I hope!

I already knew Kirk a bit before the show, and I have always thought he has two sides. One side of him is so lovely, almost too nice: the lovey-dovey family guy who loves women – he is obsessed with the whole boobs, bum and glam thing. Then there is the side of him that is like 'my way or the high-way'. He will argue himself into a big row if he thinks he's right, even though sometimes it's so blatantly obvious that he is wrong. I keep out of all that; I don't want to get on his wrong side, knowing

I already knew Kirk a bit before the show, and I have always thought he had two sides

what he can be like. We're not close, but we will probably always be in the same group of friends.

Anyway, once Brian had got a taste of fame he definitely wanted to keep working in TV, and he came up with this idea that he wanted to do a show about Essex. He wanted it to be like the American show *The Hills*, but with people from here. Because he's from Essex himself, he knew it would be a bit mad and would show how different the place is from anywhere else in the UK. Or, for that matter, from anywhere in the world!

So he told us this plan, and said he wanted to call the show *Totally Essex* and make a pilot, a one-off version of the show that you give to production companies to see if you can get anyone interested in making it. He asked if the three of us wanted to be in it. I've never asked why he specifically wanted me to do it, but I guess he thought I was a good fun girl who is down to earth but likes to party too – pretty much what Essex is about.

At the time, as I've said, it wasn't really in my life plan, but

I thought, 'Well, I have nothing to lose, so why not?' Actually I thought nothing big would really come of it, other than if I was on TV, it would probably be quite good for my modelling career. So I reckoned I would go for it.

So Brian invited me, Amy, Kirk and a few of his other friends who he thought would make for funny TV over to his friend Chris Carter's house. Chris was also taking part in the pilot show, and Mark Wright was there too. I had known Mark for a few years, and he was popular and well known in the area, partly for all his club work, but also as a playboy – yep, even before *TOWIE* was aired, that was definitely his local reputation! So I guess Brian knew he'd make good viewing.

There was a TV company called Sassy Productions on board too, and basically for the pilot, we all had to talk about ourselves to camera: what we did for a living, why we loved our lives, what set Essex apart from the rest of the country, that kind of thing. I talked mostly about doing glamour modelling. Looking back at the tape, it is so embarrassing and cringey – if that had been aired, it might have been the biggest mistake of my life!

Mark chatted to camera about how good-looking he was, that kind of thing – typical of him

Mark chatted to camera about how he was so good-looking that he would never go home alone, that kind of thing – typical of him. He kept winking at the camera and his hair was slicked back with tons of gel – it was really funny. Kirk talked a lot about how much money he had and about clubbing, and Amy talked about her boob job and basically just chatted on in the way she does. I don't know if I should admit this, but you can still find the pilot on YouTube . . .

To be honest, I don't think any of us came across particularly well.

You can still find the pilot somewhere on YouTube. . .

Then Brian went off with the tape, and we heard nothing about it for just under a year. He was going to production companies, but it seemed no one wanted it, which may have been a good thing!

Anyhow, the next thing that happened – I was 19 by now – was I got a call from a lady called Sarah Dillistone from Lime Pictures, who said she wanted to meet me and Amy for a casting for a new show she was doing. We went together to Mooro's, a restaurant in Chigwell, next to the gym where Amy used to work as a beautician, and just chatted with her. It was really relaxed, and at the end she was basically like 'I love you'. We found out later that she had also seen Mark and Kirk, and we were like 'Oh my God, this is amazing!'

I've know Arg for years, we get on brilliantly, although we argue like brother and sister

They also got James Argent – Arg – on board through Mark. I have known Arg for years after I dated one of his friends, and I think he is a great guy. We get on brilliantly, although we argue like brother and sister. He knows I will always be straight with him and tell him when he is annoying me, and he doesn't always like that and tells me I am horrible, but both of us know the other one doesn't mean it. It's a classic brother–sister relationship.

I had my first ciggie with Arg. He used to smoke the odd cheeky cigarette, and when I was about 18 I remember having one with him at a bus stop. It makes me laugh thinking of that. I liked hanging out with Arg, but I didn't like the cigarette!

Anyway, as well as Arg, Mark got his then girlfriend Lauren Goodger and his sister Jess Wright on board. Harry Derbidge came through me and Amy, and then there was a couple who appeared only in the first series, Candy Jacobs and Michael Woods. And that was about it – the cast (if that's what you could call us!) wasn't so big in the beginning.

Harry is Amy's cousin, but I have known him since he was six, when he would come to family meals, and even then it was pretty obvious he was gay – Amy was always putting shoes and make-up on him and doing him up like a doll. His brother is very blokeish, so I think he's always enjoyed having me and Amy around to talk to.

He confronted and dealt with the fact that he was gay really well. I think his family – especially his mum Karen, who is lovely – gave him loads of support. He was openly gay through school, and his attitude was: 'This is who I am, I can't help being this way, deal with it.' And I think because he was so brave and was not worried about what other people thought, he didn't get any hassle. What you see is what you get with Harry. He is obsessed with everything to do with girls, like boobs and periods. We all knew he would make for great TV!

Anyway, we did a pilot with Lime, and this time it was exactly as *TOWIE* turned out. So rather than talking to camera, as we had done with Brian, it was us being filmed actually getting on with everyday life. We weren't given much of a brief at all, as I think at this point the producers wanted to just let us get on with it and see what happened. So they would say things like: 'Just get ready for a night out and chat with each other like you would if we weren't here.'

A lot of the scenes from the pilot ended up in the first episode, like us taking Amy's dog for a walk and me and Amy getting ready for a night at Sugar Hut. It was so weird having the cameras there as we got on with our normal lives. They try to make it as subtle as possible, but at the end of the day there are a lot of people involved in filming, so it can end up feeling more like a set, no matter how hard they try. There are usually about ten people, including three cameramen with cameras on tripods, a sound guy, a director and a producer.

I remember the very first scene we filmed really clearly. It was the one I mentioned in the introduction, with me, Amy and Harry in the shop, when Amy came out of the changing room in a wedding dress. Oh my God, it was hilarious. The moment that marked

A lot of the scenes from the pilot ended up in the first episode, like me getting vajazzled and me and Amy getting ready for a night out in Sugar Hut

They try to make it as subtle as possible, but it can end up feeling like a set no matter how hard they try

the point of no return in our laughing was when I said to Amy, 'Oh, Kirk will definitely take you up the aisle.' I meant it innocently, but all three of us have dirty minds and we got the giggles and were soon hysterical. The crew didn't get the innuendo and got the hump with us, but we were lying on the floor laughing. We really couldn't get it together, and they were like, 'Come on.' But this was all so new to us – we just couldn't take it too seriously.

As Amy Childs came out through the changing room curtain in a wedding dress, I felt a nervous giggle building up in me

They couldn't use that bit, but the idea is to try not to reshoot any scenes, because that wouldn't be natural. You might have to repeat a sentence for the camera, if someone talks over you, or repeat a walk down the stairs or something if they got the angle wrong, but most of the time reshooting wouldn't work, because you wouldn't get people's genuine reactions. Anyway, that first day of filming was great, and no wonder the pilot was so good!

I am not really sure what happened as far as Brian was concerned. We didn't fall out with him, as he accepts that Amy and I were approached by a different company, who we saw as bringing in a new project. But he claims

The idea is to try and not reshoot any scenes because that wouldn't be natural

that the idea was stolen from him by Lime Pictures, and Lime claim they were already working on a very similar concept, but also say that we did come to their attention through Brian's tape. I don't know the ins and outs really, but I know it has now become a legal battle between them, as was reported in the papers last year (2011), which is a shame.

I think Brian is upset as he got no credit for bringing the main characters to the table, and to be fair I am not sure Lime would have found me and Amy without him. Kirk and Mark are maybe a different matter though, as they were so well known around Essex that anyone wanting to do a show about life there would probably have ended up finding them.

Either way, it was a brilliant idea, whoever came up with it first. But I am glad we ended up doing the show with Lime. I love Sarah and get on really well with her, and I honestly don't think – much as I love Brian – that he would have pulled off a better show, even for such simple reasons like him obviously having a much smaller budget to work with. Lime has been great to work with, and the whole crew have definitely become genuinely good friends of mine now.

Anyway, there was a gap of only a month or two after we filmed the pilot before Lime took it to ITV2. I have no idea what was said about it and what made them decide to go for it, but ITV obviously liked it, because soon after Sarah called to tell us it had been commissioned. I really didn't know at that point what *TOWIE* was going to turn into, but I tell you, I was so excited at the time anyway. I just remember leaping around the house, and Amy and I making all sorts of crazy plans for what we would do when we became well known. We loved the idea of posing for the paparazzi! I didn't think twice about handing in my notice at the bank as soon as it was commissioned – come on, it was hardly a difficult choice, was it? It didn't occur to me to take on an agent at this point – it was only halfway through the first series, when people started approaching me to do interviews and photo shoots, that I realised I needed someone to look after that side of things.

There was a bit more filming to be done to finish off the first episode, but we didn't do anything for later episodes just yet, as they wanted to keep it as current as possible. So what you see on TV each week has generally been filmed within the last week. Once they had enough material for the first episode, they invited the cast to the Maddox Club in London for the official launch – and I cannot tell you how excited we were.

I didn't think twice about handing in my notice at the bank as soon as it was commissioned – it was hardly a difficult choice, was it?

We got there and there were posters of us all over the place, and all the top people from ITV. They were basically the big bosses who had decided the show would happen. There was also loads of press there to meet us for the first time and watch the first episode, which was so scary, as what the media think of something can really influence the public.

It was the first big event I had to go to in my role on the TV show, and it was so exciting. I remember I had my hair all blow-dried and was wearing a cream dress from ASOS that was short at the front and long at the back. It took me ages to decide on my outfit, but I think I made the right call in the end. Back then I had to pay for my clothes, just like everyone else, and I still can't quite believe how lucky I am to get some of my outfits for free these days.

Until then I'd always got the train to go into London, but this time they sent cars for us, which in itself made me feel amazing, and nearly like a celebrity. I remember I shared a car with Amy and Kirk and, oh my God, it's hard to describe how weird it was for us. We were all so nervous, but also giddy with excitement – we had no idea where this TV show was going to take us, but we were up for giving it a go!

> They sent cars for us ... it's hard to describe how weird it was for us. We were all so nervous

When we got to the club, I remember we were all doing our best to be on perfect behaviour. We were so worried what the journalists would write about us and the show – we really wanted them to put positive reviews in their newspapers and magazines.

So we had a meet and greet with them in an upstairs room, where they asked us lots of questions. It was weird for us, and it can't have been easy for them either, as at that point they didn't know anything about us, so the questions were very general, like what the best thing about Essex was and whether we were all single. I can remember Amy and Kirk being really flirty, and she kept joking that she was going to marry him. That is the kind of silly thing that she would never say now because while it seems funny at the time, it can look quite different in print. Nowadays we are all a lot more guarded about what we say to the media, but that day everyone just said whatever came into their heads.

Then everyone else went downstairs to see a screening of the first episode. And do you know what? We weren't allowed down there! We had to sit upstairs and wait. And, oh my God, we were soooo nervous. We attempted to make conversation, but really we were just trying to listen out for any signs from downstairs. Luckily though, all we heard was laughter, and we kept telling each other that was at least a good sign.

Nowadays we are all a lot more guarded about what we say to the media but that day everyone just said what came into their heads

The screening was an hour long, and it felt like a very long hour, I can tell you. But finally everyone came upstairs and were like, 'Well done, we loved it, we can't believe how funny it was. It will be amazing.'

It was such a relief to see their response, and quite motivating too. It was probably only at that point that everyone realised for the first time: 'Hold on, this show we are getting involved in might actually work and be quite big.' I had no idea what to expect from the next few months, I just knew I was so happy to be involved, and I loved the idea of the new things that it could bring.

Sarah was great. She really took the show on as her project, and looked after the cast really well. She would come round to the house just for a gossip and a cup of tea and would stay for like three hours. She would come to talk to me about coping with the media and the attention and to keep me up to date about what was going on – and also I reckon so she knew exactly what was happening in my life. That way she could decide which bits would be the most interesting to film. The idea is that the *TOWIE* producers always know exactly what is going on with you, so if I thought I fancied someone, or I was really mad at someone, I'd tell them.

The idea is that the TOWIE producers always know exactly what is going on with you

Sadly Sarah only worked on *TOWIE* for series one – and then went off to be a producer on *Made in Chelsea*. Can you believe she dropped us for that show?! I guess she was offered more money though, and I don't blame them for wanting her – she is really good at her job and we were sad to see her go. I do actually like *Made in Chelsea* too. It's weird, because it is like a different world from Essex, but at the same time they go through a lot of the same things as us. I always say though, no matter how good it is, *TOWIE* is still the best!

The way filming works is that we are told how many weeks the show will be on for, and we have to keep those free, while still living our normal lives, if you get what I mean. So, for example, if I am told to keep ten weeks free from the start of September, I can't go booking any holidays or making any big plans in that time.

The way filming works is that we are told how many weeks the show will be on for

While we get on with life as normal, we also have to allow for what they want to film. That

13

takes priority over anything else for those ten weeks. So say I want to go and visit a friend in London, but it is not something the producers want to film and they decide they need footage of me in Minnies, I have to cancel my friend and go to Minnies. And the hardest thing is that we only get told the night before whether we are needed the next day and at what times. So life definitely revolves around *TOWIE* for those ten weeks. I'm not having a moan about it though – it is my job really and I love it! Luckily I'm still close to my old friends, and they are all really understanding when and if I have to cancel on them. I always try to rearrange our plans and make it up to them by passing on some of the freebies I get sent.

Of all three series we have done, the first one was my favourite to film. We just had so much fun. You know when you start at school and you are making new friends and learning new things and everything is fresh and exciting? Well it was like that at the beginning. And we weren't known yet, so looking good in case the paps were around wasn't an issue. Things like whether the bit we were filming might annoy people and we would get abuse for it on Twitter hadn't occurred to us yet, so we were just totally enjoying ourselves and having a mad time. Sorry to be all sentimental – because, don't get me wrong, I have loved filming every series since – but I guess I just look back on it as being a time of innocence or something, kind of like you look at your junior school days in a 'wasn't it nice' sort of way.

Seriously, Amy, Harry and I had the best time filming together in the salon. We would get self-conscious when we suddenly remembered the cameras were there, or just make ourselves hysterical so that we'd cry with laughter. It took us a while to learn how to ignore the cameras and behave naturally, but now it's pretty much second nature to us.

We didn't plan what we would do or say – that was just us. I think you can see everyone's true colours most clearly in series one. You see Lauren really out of control, you see Mark and his 'she's fit' comments, and as for Amy ... I know some people questioned whether she was acting or given lines, but, believe me, that was the real Amy! The funny, sweet, lovely, say-anything-that-pops-into-her-head girl who was my best friend from school. It's definitely more the real her than the Amy we saw on her solo show *It's All About Amy*, where I could see that everything she was saying and doing was too thought out for the cameras, whether she knew it or not. Maybe that's why a second series wasn't commissioned.

It took us a while to learn how to ignore the cameras and behave naturally

When you look at how everyone else became a part of the show – they all pretty much came about because of a link with me, Amy, Kirk or Mark. We are the original four, definitely. As far as people I brought in, obviously my sister Billie was through me. Then I introduced Lucy Mecklenburgh – Lucy Meck – to Mark in

We didn't plan what we would do or say – that was just us. I think you can see everyone's true colours most clearly in series one

Marbella just before we filmed series one. So as soon as he was single and able to make a move, that was her lined up for *TOWIE*, as anyone Mark got involved with was going to become central to the show.

I mentioned to the bosses I knew Peri Sinclair, who had the shop around the corner. And then Joey got onto the show because of me – although he will never admit it! He got papped with me on a night out once and I told the photographers his name was Joey Essex, and they loved that cos you couldn't make it up – but no one thought it was his real surname. I told the producers to put him on the show, and then I ended up getting with him. And because of the link to me he got lots of air time, which showcased how entertaining he can be. Like when he took me on a date and we ended up visiting a tip and then eating these squashed sandwiches in the middle of the woods. It was pure genius, and really established him as a central character. He will never ever thank me for it, but look at those facts!

In fact, thinking about it, I need to get some commission off all this lot! Of course, I wasn't the only one from the original *TOWIE* lot who made suggestions to the producers, and I'm sure that each and every one of us thinks that we were the one who brought the most to the table!

2

THE ORANGE COUNTY RULES

When I was young, I was a bit of a letdown as far as the Essex girl image goes because I don't remember being that interested in beauty in my early years. I was a proper tomboy throughout primary school, and was never one of those little girls that worry about their looks and spend hours looking in the mirror and trying on their mums' make-up. And I think that is partly a way of thinking that I got from my mum Sue.

When I was young, I was a bit of a letdown as far as the Essex girl image goes

Don't get me wrong, Mum definitely knows how to look good – she is glam, stylish and totally gorgeous! She is also a really young mum – she had me when she was just 22 years old. But she doesn't go in for fake tans, false nails, or anything like that. She was more bothered about being a mum – things like putting a good dinner on the table for us all every night when Billie and I were growing up – rather than looking like she had walked straight out of the salon.

So it was only really when I went to secondary school, and the other girls began to get into beauty routines and that, that I learned about it and started getting into it too. I wasn't obsessively girly or anything, but I started to take a lot more interest in my appearance, and enjoyed experimenting with the latest crazes along with all my friends.

I went to Shenfield High School when I was 11. It is a pretty nice school in Shenfield, which is just outside of Brentwood. It is a mixed school, but the boys and girls are taught separately which, looking back, is a good idea – it meant we were less distracted in class! I guess it must work, as the school gets pretty good results. Billie is 11 months older than me, and was in the year above me at school. Mum would give us a lift in every day and I'd say I was pretty happy there. I wasn't too bothered about the academic side of things, but I loved the socialising and the friends and the fun times. Mum was fine with the fact that I wasn't very academic, as long as she knew that I wasn't wasting my education and was making the best of things in my own way.

At school there was a group of seven of us who were all best friends. Lucy Meck was one of them, which shows how long we have been friends

At school there was a group of seven of us who were all best friends. Lucy Meck was one of them, which shows just how long we have been friends, although I admit we aren't as close now as we were then, as you might have noticed … The seven of us hung around together all the time, and I'm not going to lie – we were the popular girls in school. We called ourselves the Seven Sexy Cinders, after Cinderella. We came up with the name ourselves and were pretty pleased with it! So pleased we made a book about ourselves, which I've still got. It is full of photos of us all posing and having fun, and notes that we wrote each other about our nights out, and of course the boys we fancied, and our plans to always stay best friends. It's definitely a book of great memories that I am going to keep forever – even if some of the things in it are a bit embarrassing to read now!

But although we were popular, we weren't like something out of the *Mean Girls* movie or anything like that. We weren't nasty, and I got on with everyone in my year. I remember one girl called Heather who I used to sit next to in German class. She hated the glam look and wasn't interested in celebrities and that, but we always used to chat and have a laugh. I didn't judge her for being different from me. That's something I have always tried to stick to – everyone chooses their own way to act and look, and if it doesn't hurt anyone, just because it is different from how I choose to portray myself, it doesn't mean I will judge them because of it.

Billie was in the year above me at school, and she was in a group of friends that called themselves the Shenna Plasticz. I looked up to her and her friends a lot, and we started changing our appearance and using beauty products around the same time. As I've said, it wasn't that I suddenly became obsessed about the way I looked, but it was really good fun to try out new products and beauty routines, and I think that's pretty normal for a lot of girls our age. But our mum and grandparents used to get mad at us for our make-up, and especially the fake tan.

I remember my Nana Liz, Mum's mum, who still lives near us in Brentwood, saying, 'Your skin is so lovely, why are you girls putting that tan on it?' But we didn't want to know – we were sure we looked good!

In the year above me were a group of girls we called the Orange Crew'

In the year above me were a group of girls we called the Orange Crew. And, oh my God, they had proper bleached-white hair, orange skin and false eyelashes. When we first started at the school we thought they looked silly, but a year later things changed and we were starting to look the same! I don't think we did it to such an extreme – a lot of us still had dark hair rather than white-blonde – but we definitely had the orange faces and the lip gloss. I love lip gloss; I became obsessed with it then and am obsessed with it now. It is definitely one of my must-have beauty items.

I love lip gloss, I became obsessed with it then and am obsessed with it now. It is one of my must-have beauty items

Not everyone in our year went through the same transformation obviously. Some girls took it too far, and some didn't care and wouldn't do anything about their looks at all, but we went for glam and pretty, and I like to think we got it about right. But you can be the judge of that – have a look at the photo on page 2 in the picture section.

It's weird when you look back. One day you are looking all sweet and innocent and childlike, then the next you discover all this beauty stuff and your whole appearance really changes. But it is all part of growing up, and I definitely think people need to try things out when they are teenagers – you just need to accept that you will get some of it wrong and will not always be happy to look back at the photos!

So anyway, an Essex girl will try to make sure she looks good all the time, but especially on nights out. We like a glamorous, big, full-on look that catches people's attention, and we are not afraid to look like we have made a lot of effort – why should you hide the fact that you want to look the best you can? That's a good thing!

But that takes time. Before a night out I will take on average two hours to get ready – and that is assuming all the other stuff like my nails and tan are already done. I like to get ready with my mates, at my house, with a glass of wine and some music in the background to get us in the mood. If I absolutely had to though, like if I had no warning I was going out, I could get ready in an hour, but that really would be the quickest. I would rather not go out at all if I had less time than that.

Before a night out we will take on average two hours to get ready

As everyone knows, the tan is probably the most important thing for an Essex girl. There is a reason Essex is nicknamed the Orange County! But we are proud of it, and looking tanned means you also look healthier and slimmer. Not that I always got it right from the start . . .

The first time I tried fake tan was when I was about 14. I can't remember exactly who out of the Seven Sexy Cinders started it first, but suddenly it was something we were all doing. Last year, Lucy tweeted a picture of me and her at the age of 13, lying on the grass looking really tanned, and the press picked it up and ran a story implying we used fake tan even back then. But actually we had just been on a camping trip and were both naturally brown – it was a year later that we hit the fake tan for the first time.

As everyone knows, the tan is probably the most important thing for an Essex girl!

But yeah, when we started getting into it, we got 100 per cent into it, and keeping up our tans became a really important thing. The downside of that, of course, was that when we got it wrong, we got it 100 per cent wrong, but we didn't care – it was all about the tan! We were using these tanning wipes you could get from Superdrug for 99p, and we used them *all* the time after that, even though we didn't really know what we were doing. We would end up looking orange, like *really* orange – especially our hands. We used to get these dark-orange marks between our fingers, which was a total giveaway, so that everyone knew what we had been doing.

It didn't go down well with the teachers. They noticed what

we were doing and used to tell us off. But we never took any notice really. I mean, seriously, what kid takes style tips from their teacher? In fact, our rule was that the more they hated our look, the more we loved it.

I have pretty much been tanned ever since, though obviously I have moved on from the tanning wipes. Now I do my own tan at home with a can of Fake Bake. It costs about £30, and I put two layers on all over me each time, so each can lasts for around four uses. But while I'm pretty expert at doing it now, if it is a special occasion I'll go down to the salon to have it done, as there is still always the chance of screwing it up. They are professionals, so it is always going to be that bit better. I like Fake Bake as a brand, as I don't think it is as sticky as some of the others – that sticky feeling you get after you have put the stuff on but before you can wash it off is horrible with some of the products. And while all tanning products smell a bit, the smell of Fake Bake isn't as bad as most of them.

Being tanned is like a religion in Essex. Pretty much everyone does it, and I don't just mean the girls, but the boys too. Personally I think pale skin can be nice, if it's like porcelain with freckles – whatever makes you happy really, but I do think tanned is the best. Luckily my skin is quite naturally olive coloured, which helps when you fake tan a lot and, to be honest, it just makes me feel more confident in my appearance.

So yeah, while being tanned is still pretty much a must for an Essex girl, we are realising the risks and choosing to go for the fake. Girls will get a spray tan done every week –

it's set in the diary like a weekly appointment, like church used to be in the old days, but now it's less God and more Goddess!

Even though not many girls are using sunbeds these days, for obvious reasons, boys still make the most of them. In fact you will find more boys on the sunbeds these days than girls in Essex. All the boys on *TOWIE* are doing it. I think they want to be tanned, but they reckon getting a spray tan or using cream is too girly, so they go on the beds. Somehow they think doing it that way is manlier. Except Harry Derbidge of course – he loves a good spray tan! I can't remember the last time I had a sunbed – I think about my skin too much to risk that.

Harry Derbidge loves a good spray tan!

My forehead has peeled a couple of times when I have been burned in the sun, and it is really bad. I don't like that. But I do love the heat and the sun and lying on the beach while on holiday, so the whole risk thing can be a proper dilemma. I whack factor 15 all over my body, and factor 30 on my face – I especially worry about the skin on my face, as I 100 per cent don't want to get wrinkles just yet!

When Billie and I were young we got called the Jetsetters at school, because we were always on holiday and would come back with tans when everyone else was looking white and pasty, which was amazing! My grandparents on my biological dad's side, Wendy and Mick, live in Spain, and my parents owned a place in Alicante for a while, so we used to go out there all the time during the school holidays and would come

24

back with good tans. I'd do my best to make my tan last by moisturising loads, so it would fade slower.

We even lived in Alicante for a while – for about five months when I was 15. That was enough time for us to get really brown. We don't have the place out there anymore, but I'd like to own somewhere abroad one day if possible.

The downside of all this fake tanning, of course, is that Essex girls have orange-stained beds once a week. The reason for that is the day you get it done you need to leave it for about eight hours, so we will get the spray done in the afternoon or evening, sleep in it, and then shower it off in the morning. But through the night some of the tan will rub off onto the sheets and duvet. It's not the nicest thing in the world, but it's something any boyfriend of an Essex girl has to get used to. Nowadays you can get bed protectors to stop it from happening – you clip them onto your sheets like a sleeping bag. I have one and have tried using it, but I reckon it is a lot of effort. I think only the really hardcore tanners use them, and actually it's just better not to have your best sheets on your bed that one night of the week.

So that is the skin all sorted. Also massively important for an Essex girl's beauty routine is nails – no one likes to see bitten or short unpainted nails. I think the best way to keep them looking good is to go false.

I think I discovered fake nails about a year after learning the importance of a tan, when I was around 15. I'd always played around with nail polishes, but it was in Year 11 at school that me and the girls discovered acrylic nails. We'd go to the local Chinese nail shop and get them done for £20 – or cheaper if you were a student. It still added up though, in those days, and looking back at those really long nails with their white tips now, I think they were so tacky and a waste of our money!

As well as looking tacky, the way they were applied couldn't have done our nails much good. You would go into the salon and sit down, trying not to mind that really strong chemical smell you get in those shops, and there would be all these random electric tools they would use on you. It's like half your nail got filed away to make way for the acrylic. Then your nails would get even more damaged while the acrylic ones were on, so you thought you'd have to keep using the fake ones to cover it up. It was a hard cycle to break.

After about a year I got tired of those nails, and decided they didn't look so good after all, so I stopped using them and just put nail polish on myself. It was only when I started doing glamour modelling when I was 18 that I began looking for a different way to keep my nails looking good again, and I discovered Bio Sculpture Gel – and that is definitely what I would recommend now.

How it works is that I get a coloured gel put over my own nails, and then a clear gel over the top of that. It hardens into a really tough but quite natural-looking nail which lasts for a month and never chips. It is particularly good because my nails just get a quick file and buff first – the beautician doesn't get rid of half your own nail, so it is not so bad for them as acrylics. It is actually supposed to make your nails stronger, and is really good for anyone who bites their nails, as basically the gel is so tough that you can't.

It annoys me when I see people who don't take care of their

nails properly. I think it's so important to pay attention to details like your nails in order to make a good impression on people, especially if you have a job that involves dealing with others on a day-to-day basis, like I have in my shop, Minnies, and before that when I was a cashier in a bank. I used to sit behind the counter and deal with the customers, and it was really important to me that my hands looked good.

I've been going to the same beautician since I first discovered Bio Sculpture Gel. I go about once a month to get my nails and toenails done, then every few months I have them taken off for a week to let my nails breathe. Of course I pay for my treatments, not least because I know my nail technician is really talented, so I would rather stick with her. I believe in being loyal to people who have been good to me for ages – not just those who have been good to me once I started being on TV.

Another thing I spend a lot of time on in my beauty routine is hair removal – I am naturally really hairy! As soon as I shave my legs or bikini line (and yes, everyone asks, and it's a Hollywood for me, which means I get rid of all the hair) it grows back the next day – really annoying! I prefer to shave, as I can't afford the time it takes for it to grow back to the length you need to wax it – I am always on a shoot, or the beach, or doing something where people would see my stubble, so I have to get rid of it as soon as it appears. Venus razors all the way for me.

As for my teeth, I am pretty happy with how they look. I obsessively clean them – there is no way I can go on a night out without doing it – and I use Pearl Drops Replenishing

White Toothpaste at the moment. My teeth are naturally quite white and straight, and I have been lucky enough never to have had to wear braces.

But when the show started I began to notice that some people's teeth were positively glowing on screen. So when I was offered the chance to have them done for free during the first series I was like 'Yeah, let's do it.' It was a Zoom! treatment, where they put whitening gel on my teeth and then I sat with a light shining onto them for 45 minutes, which somehow works with the gel to get rid of stains and darker bits of colour. But I have to say it killed. My teeth really hurt for the next 24 hours.

You can see me getting them done on the show, while Amy and Harry take the piss, and as I can't talk with the stuff in my mouth, I just have to write them a note saying it was tingling. But that was an understatement! To be fair, it made a bit of difference to the colour, but it was more like they just got a good clean, and I'm not sure it was worth the pain. Not that it stopped me trying it again. I went to the Harley Street Smile Clinic, but this time I only lasted ten minutes before the pain got too much. I think my teeth must be too sensitive, so there will be no third time! The things us girls do in the name of beauty! Generally though, I am pretty happy within myself these days. I'm not saying I think I'm a ten out of ten – everyone has things they want to change about themselves – but I am mostly happy with how I look.

I'm not against surgery, but it isn't something I'd consider having now

I'm not against surgery, but it is not something that I'd consider having now. Weirdly though, when the show started, some people thought I had had some work done, probably because of the stereotype that everyone in Essex has had something done, and because my eyes are such an unusual shape that they assume I've had a lift or something. But for the record, I 100 per cent have never had surgery. It bothered me a bit when I read people's comments about it online, but I got really upset when *heat* magazine did a piece about celebrity surgery and quoted a so-called 'expert' who said he thought I had had surgery.

I felt horrible that it had appeared in the magazine for everyone to read – and it wasn't even true! I didn't understand why they hadn't called me to check their facts, or at least get my side of it. Instead I only knew about it when I saw it in the magazine. It was one of the first negative stories that were written about me, and not one I will forget. It really put me off working with that magazine for a while, as I felt like it was a real invasion. It has also obviously stuck in other people's minds, as I still get asked about it even now. I'll talk more about the negative effects of some of the press I've had later, but this was my first real wake-up call about the downsides of being in the public eye.

But I guess I am one of the few girls on the show who hasn't had surgery. I think out of the main cast, it is just me, Billie and Lydia who have avoided having any so far. Everyone else has had something done. They are all really open about it – I think it is the culture now to just say if you have had it done. It's not something to be embarrassed about, it is just another thing you are doing to look better. On set during series three, Maria was talking about how she wanted lipo. That seems crazy to me, as she doesn't have any fat on her, but I guess if she wants it … And Chloe was quite open, even on screen, about wanting bum implants. Especially given that she has had a baby, that girl has an amazing figure. She is such a lovely girl, and I just don't know why she'd even consider the kind of surgery she says she wants.

I just think that at my age, if it's not broken, don't try and fix it. But maybe when I've had kids I'll want my boobs done if they have gone droopy, and if that's what I feel then, I'll go for it. As for Botox, all the girls on *TOWIE* sit around discussing when their next appointment is. For me, it's not right – smile lines and dimples are part of your character, and Botox can make people look too scary, especially if they have it done at a young age.

Botox can make people look too scary, especially if they have it done at a young age

I reckon that kind of thing is where girls go wrong. They think boys will like it, but actually if you really try to get to the bottom of what boys want, they generally prefer girls to look more natural. Not that anyone should become obsessed with what boys like. Making the best of your looks should be about doing it for YOU, to boost your own confidence and make you feel good about yourself.

I read somewhere that the number of enquiries about plastic surgery shot up after *TOWIE* started, especially in the Essex area, which is bad! Apparently clinics could even see that more people were logging onto their websites to look at treatments while the show was on air. It's crazy, and I think people should be happy with how they look, rather than trying to look like a celebrity. Then again, if someone thinks I look so good that they want to copy me, I am only going to take that as a compliment!

My Ten Steps to the Perfect Tan

Tanning is really quite simple once you get your routine right, but if you don't, streaks and patches can be a nightmare. This is how I do mine. There are obviously other ways, but I reckon if you follow this, you should be able to do a pretty good job at home:

1. Exfoliate around your elbows, knees and ankles, to get rid of any dead skin.

2. Moisturise those areas, but only really lightly, with a tiny bit of cream. Also rub a tiny bit onto your wrists – orange wrists are a dead giveaway.

3. Spray yourself all over with a can of Fake Bake spray. You can use a cream, but I prefer the light spray of the can, as I think it looks more natural. Follow the instructions on the can. You will only learn through practice how much works for you – one layer will give a light, natural tan, but I tend to do two coats for a bit of a darker colour.

4. When you do your face, use less than you would on your body. It is better for your face to be a bit lighter – you can darken it up with make-up if you need to.

5. It's definitely worth investing in a mitt, which you put on your hand and rub over the tan. This makes sure it is really evenly spread, and stops you getting orange hands.

6. Despite the mitt, still wash your hands as some of the fake tan can soak through. Then spray very lightly over the back of your hands. Orange hands are a no-no, but white hands are nearly as bad!

7. Then give the tan time to dry – I'd say ten minutes would be the minimum – before putting on something old that you don't mind getting fake tan on. I have an old, slouchy pyjama top that I always wear afterwards.

8. Leave the tan on for eight hours minimum before washing it off. This is why I like doing it on an evening in, then washing it off in the morning. It will look too dark and streaky that evening, but develops nicely overnight into a perfect glow for the morning. Make sure you wash it all off properly

though – it's amazing how many girls I see with streaks on them days later because it didn't all come off in the shower.

9. Some people do this routine weekly, but I tend to go for ten days to two weeks. To make it last, moisturise every day after your shower, as the tan makes your skin quite dry.

10. If it is a special occasion, and you want to be sure it looks good, find a good salon, and they will do a professional job. While it's more expensive, it will always be worth it.

What Is Vajazzling and Should I Do It?

Everyone asks me the same questions about vajazzling – 'What is it?' 'Did Amy Childs invent it?' and 'Does every girl in Essex get it done?'

The truth, as far as I know, is that it was big in America first but hadn't really made its way over to the UK. Amy had trained in beauty before we started the first

➡

series, and the producers were keen to show that side of her to viewers. They wanted to show her doing a treatment, but they were looking for a way to make it a bit funnier. Someone suggested vajazzling, and Amy had heard of it, so the scene just came about. I hadn't heard of it, but as soon as I heard the word 'vajazzling' I didn't need it explained!

But I can't believe how much it has taken off. Everyone knows what it is now, and there are salons in Essex that actually offer it alongside all the other treatments. It's so weird how huge it has become and how so many people want it done, just because we did it as a joke on the show. It's crazy and just shows the power of *TOWIE*.

To get vajazzled properly basically means the beautician sticking little diamante jewels in a pattern around your vagina with a special glue. But you can now get transfer kits that contain sticker-like jewels that you can put on yourself at home. Obviously you have to be hair-free for it to work, or they won't stick properly. They'll last about three days. I reckon it's worth going to a salon the first time to see how they do it, but then the transfers are good enough. It's all good fun!

I have actually only ever been vajazzled three times. The first time was by Amy for the show and then I did it myself at home using the transfers. I'd only ever get them done for a boyfriend though – they are not really worth doing just for yourself!

Even boys have started getting them done. The first time I saw that was when I did a PA in a club called Paparazzi in Watford and there were two salon girls vajazzling people. Boys who had had one too many drinks were getting brave and going for it, and then showing me afterwards. They were flashing on the dancefloor. It was mad!

My Getting Ready Timetable

This is generally how I spend my two hours getting ready for a night out:

7 p.m. – Take a shower, wash my hair, shave and exfoliate.

7.20 p.m. – Put my hair up in a bun and out of the way – I style it last, otherwise I'd have to put it up when done and it would get a kink in it. I usually have a mate around to get ready with, or Billie, so we'll have a glass of wine to get the night started around now.

7.30 p.m. – I will be tanned already, but I will add extra instant tan to bits of me that will be showing that night. At the minute I like using Vani-T's Bronzing Custard, or one of Soap & Glory's instant tanning products.

7.35 p.m. – Do my make-up.

8.00 p.m. – Blow-dry my hair, and then maybe curl it.

8.20 p.m. – Now I choose my outfit. This is the time-consuming bit! Like any good Essex girl, I take forever to decide, but eventually I will know what is right for the night.

8.50 p.m. – Choosing a clutch bag is always a pain for me, as there never seems to be one that exactly matches my outfit. But I'll find one and pack it with everything I need for a night out – generally my phone, money, keys, chewing gum, blusher, powder and lip gloss.

8.55 p.m. Spritz of perfume – no point having the perfect outfit and make-up if you don't smell good too! I don't have a signature scent. I'd like to one day, but for now my tastes keep changing. At the minute though my favourite is probably Chanel's Coco Mademoiselle. Chanel is the classic range that every girl needs in her collection, but this one is quite girly, not like a more mature woman's perfume. I am also loving Paco Rabanne's Lady Million and Viktor & Rolf's Flowerbomb at the moment.

9 p.m. – Finish off the bottle of wine, and we are out the door and ready for a great night!

3

I'VE ALWAYS
BEEN A POSER

Being photographed and knowing that picture of you is going to go all around the country – or even the world – is a really weird thing. The way people are with celebrities today, you know the picture will be analysed and judged in all sorts of ways: whether what I am wearing looks good or not, whether I look fat or thin, if I am with a guy, or if I look upset in any way. Not that being a celeb and being on the receiving end of that changes how you look at the pictures yourself – I still look at everyone else's pictures and make those judgements too. Although I guess maybe now I do it with a bit more knowledge of what is happening behind the scenes – how a picture might not always show

Being photographed and knowing that picture of you is going to go all around the country is a really weird thing

things exactly as they are. And of course I have a lot more understanding of how scary it can be for celebrities to be followed around by photographers who can often come across as quite aggressive when they are trying to get the shot they want.

I have always been a poser though, and a fan of cameras, and have a sixth sense about how to pose. So while getting used to being photographed since I've become a celebrity is weird, it has not been too hard.

I have always been a poser though, and a fan of cameras, and have a sixth sense about how to pose

In fact, even when I was a baby, I appeared in an advert, so I guess I started young. It was an ad for a German beer, and I was in it as the crying baby being put to bed by a man pretending to be my dad. It went on billboards around the country, which is quite funny looking back – a very early and strange start on my route to fame!

I had been put forward for the role by my mum, and I guess we must have made a bit of cash out of it. But we didn't really do any more of those kind of things after that – there was too much travelling involved, and while Mum was happy for us to do a bit of modelling and acting and that, she was not like one of those pushy pageant mums or anything. She wanted us girls to take advantage of any opportunities that came our way, but she also wanted us to have a normal, happy childhood.

We had some professional family shoots done when we were kids, to be put up around the house, of Billie and me dressed up in adults' clothes. We were just toddlers, and were dressed in blazers that were too big for us, wearing big pearl necklaces and bowler hats. They are funny, and you can see us posing and pouting already! It is great to have them, and they are a definite sign of what was to come.

Billie is actually more of a poser than me, and has been ever since we were young. Whereas I like doing quite serious poses, she does all sorts of funny and crazy ones. I prefer to look as good as I can, and she wants to make people laugh.

Billie and I always took photos growing up, and Mum has trunks full of the pictures. I love going through them all – photos are memories, and it is a good thing to have as many of those as possible. I often sit and go through them when I have some time on my own. That is probably why I still take so many photos myself. I hate the idea of forgetting the good times.

I have always had a camera – even at primary school I was taking photos. I love being behind the camera as well as in front of it. I would save up my money and buy a £2.99 disposable camera, and then when it was full up, I would have to wait to get enough of my pocket money together to be able to pay to develop it.

In a way, I miss the photos you had to get developed. It was cool to have to wait, whereas now you can see your pictures instantly and there is no sense of excitement. I have a camera now that gets rid of any blemishes, but actually it was funny in the past when you didn't know what to expect from your photos. You couldn't escape the bad ones that way!

Then, a few years ago, when I was 18, the posing for photos that was just fun for me as a kid, turned into a career move.

I left school at 16 and went straight to work, first for a company called Connexions and then for Lloyds TSB. It wasn't really what I wanted to do with my life, but I did know that I wanted to make money and gain my independence, so in that way it was great, as I got stuck straight in.

> When I turned 18, I decided I wanted to have a go at modelling, so I decided to have a go at glamour modelling

But when I turned 18, I decided I wanted to have a go at modelling. I liked the idea of fashion modelling, but I am not tall enough – I am 5 ft 6 and generally they like girls to be more like 5 ft 10. But I was told that I had the right figure, as I have boobs and curves in all the right places, so I decided to have a go at glamour modelling.

Glamour modelling basically covers any kind of modelling where the model is looking sexual or posing in a sexual way. Girls can be fully clothed in a pretty innocent pose, right through to being naked and in quite hardcore poses. I decided before I began that I didn't want to do anything extreme or that I would regret in later life, so I decided I would do underwear and topless, but nothing more.

Ironically it was actually Mark Wright who got me into it. He introduced me to a guy called Neil Dobias at Neon Management, and the two of them got me started. Neon Management are a company who look after a lot of models, and they launched Jordan's career, so at the time it seemed like the perfect place for someone who wanted to do well in that world. Neil and I swapped numbers, my friend took some photos of me in underwear, I sent them to him and we went from there.

They put me forward for the *Nuts* Babe 2009 modelling competition, where I had to send in photos which the readers voted on, and I got through to the final. At the party for the finalists my friends had made badges that said 'Vote for Sam'. JLS were at the party, straight off *X Factor*, and the boys wore the badges, which was amazing.

I ended up winning, and got to do a two-page spread in black underwear which went in *Nuts* magazine about three months later. They were a nerve-wracking few months, and other models were winding me up that it obviously wasn't a good enough shoot and had been pulled, but I was pleased with it when it was published.

Everyone at the bank thought I was mad to do it, but at work I wore a plain uniform and glasses, so none of the customers recognised me. I wasn't really that worried about getting in trouble, as I saw these two parts of my life as being completely separate.

Soon after, I switched to another modelling agency, Girl Management, and I did five different shoots through them, including *Zoo* magazine, and three Page Three shoots for the *Daily Star*. I also went to Majorca for a bikini shoot and did a calendar. I enjoyed it, but if I am honest, I didn't love it. I was confident about what I was doing, don't get me wrong, but I wasn't overwhelmed by it, and just didn't think it was for me.

The competition was insane as well – there were so many girls wanting to do it. It meant that it got really quite bitchy and competitive, but I never cared or got upset by it, as to me it was a hobby. It wasn't my whole life – I had other stuff going on – but for some of the girls it was their only income, and everything they had dreamt of, and they did get pretty full-on about it.

Glamour modelling wasn't my whole life – it was good I had another job at the bank with a steady income

It was good that I had another job with a steady income because I was able to decide what I wanted to do, rather than getting pushed into something more full-on than I was up for, just because I needed the cash. I can see how easily girls could be persuaded to 'push the boundaries' for money and the promise of fame. Having said that, there are pictures kicking around of me that I am not that keen on – and you can't escape the bad ones once they are out there!

Luckily for me, my parents were supportive of my glamour modelling. They thought the pictures I did were tastefully done and encouraged me to be proud of my body. When I did do topless shoots, Dad didn't look at them, so that never felt weird, and I don't think my grandparents even knew I was doing it.

I can see how easily girls could be persuaded to 'push the boundaries' for cash and the promise of fame

It is not something I regret – I was quite naïve at the time and it taught me about the way the world works. To be honest, it was something I had wanted to do, so if I hadn't given it a go, I would have ended up regretting it. And I think it also taught me a bit about the entertainment industry and how people can be, before I was really thrown into it with *TOWIE*. So I was probably better prepared for the attention when it came than some of the rest of the cast, and it was less of a shock for me.

Luckily my parents were supportive of my glamour modelling

One thing that takes some getting used to is how people can change towards you when you become a 'celebrity'. People who didn't give you the time of day before you were famous suddenly treat you really well and want to be your friend. A perfect example of this is the difference in the way I was treated on two shoots for the same magazine – once before I was on *TOWIE* and then on a shoot after the show had really taken off.

The first time was when I was getting established in the glamour industry, and it wasn't the nicest experience. I felt kind of ignored and unappreciated on set – as though the magazine staff thought they were doing me a favour

It's not something I regret – I was quite naïve at the time and it taught me about the way the world works

by allowing me to do the shoot and I was beneath them. The photographer, stylists and reporter were all a bit off-hand with me, and the other girls on the shoot weren't particularly friendly.

Then, after the first series of the show had gone out, I did a

Christmas shoot where I was wrapped up in a gift box. Anyway, I was treated very differently that time. Everyone was really friendly and nice, and went out of their way to make me feel at home and more comfortable. Even the editor called in to say hello. It was such a difference, and shows what being on TV can do.

So although it is a good thing for me at the moment because of where I am at, I do struggle with the fact that it can feel so fake. I always try to be nice to everyone, from runners to producers. I'll say please and thank you, and I know it is a cliché, but I take the attitude that I want to treat people the way I would like to be treated. I do it for two reasons. On the one hand I do it just because that is how everyone should be, but also because I want to be more farsighted than the people on that first magazine shoot were – who knows whether a runner on *TOWIE* will be the producer of a future series I may want to be part of? I want them to remember me as someone who was professional and friendly to work with, so they'll want to hire me again.

That shoot with me coming out of the box was the last topless shoot I did, as I realised glamour modelling wasn't really the thing for me, and I just wasn't getting the buzz out of it that I expected. Although I realised that *TOWIE* has quite a lot of young fans, and I didn't want to set a bad example to them, I

> I always try to be nice to everyone, from runners to producers. I know it's a cliché, but I treat people the way I would like to be treated

wouldn't have continued with the modelling for much longer, even if *TOWIE* hadn't come up. As I said, I don't regret it, and it was a good learning curve, but I wanted to move on from it.

I also think girls wanting to go down that route should be aware of how badly it pays. There are thousands of girls now who want to get into it, so the pay rates have really dropped, unless you are one of the absolute top models. There is an idea that you get tens of thou-

TOWIE has a lot of young fans and I didn't want to set a bad example to them

sands for a shoot, but the reality is that for a two-page spread you might get £250, or maybe between £800 and £1,000 for an eight-page spread. Then your agent's fees, travel expenses and any hotel bills come out of that, and there is actually a lot of work involved. So before you know it, you are not really earning that much. So anyone read-

I wouldn't have continued with the modelling for much longer, even if TOWIE hadn't come up

ing this and thinking of trying to go down that route, please keep in mind that it won't make you a millionaire!

Because of my glamour modelling experience, I now feel quite comfortable and confident when I do promotional shoots for the show or magazine shoots. We are wearing more clothes than I used to before, so I don't feel I have to be holding my figure in – I just pose! And I love checking out the end product in the newspaper or magazine.

I think you can tell who on *TOWIE* has modelled before, as they are the ones who look more relaxed. You can tell Amy wasn't comfortable posing at first, and tried too hard. She always pouted, but way too much. One day I taught her to smile instead, which was quite funny, but she genuinely looked so much better. It's like Victoria Beckham – she is beautiful, but she always pouts, whereas she looks so much prettier when she smiles, and Amy is the same.

I clearly remember the very first time I was papped after I joined *TOWIE*. As you all know, papping is basically when a photographer takes a picture of you out and about, that you didn't expect to be taken and didn't pose up for, like for example, when I am going shopping, or leaving my house, or coming out of a club. It is very different from the organised studio photo shoots.

So yes, this first time, Amy, Harry and I had been invited to a club in London called Funky Buddha for a party for Playboy Energy Drink. Kelly Brook was launching it, and Nicole Scherzinger was there. We were really excited and had spent ages getting ready. We were papped by photographers as we arrived, which was great – but then the club wouldn't let Harry in! They said it was club policy, as he wasn't 18. I was so mad, as the organisers had known his age when they invited him, and we had gone all the way from Essex to west London. I was arguing with the doorman, as it was out of

I clearly remember the very first time I was papped after I joined TOWIE

order, but it didn't work, and I tweeted afterwards, saying how dare they treat us like that. It went in the papers the next day as 'Back to Essex You Go – Essex Girls Get Turned Away', which was just rubbish! It was so embarrassing, and didn't explain at all what had happened. So it is fair to say that my first getting-papped experience wasn't that great ...

Luckily the second time I got pictured for the papers was at my first real experience of a red carpet, where the press are there to see you – and it was a much better experience. Amy and I went to the premiere of *Call of Duty* with Candy and Michael.

Call of Duty is an army video game, so as we arrived at the venue we were offered a chance to put on army-type camouflage face paint. Amy and I were like 'Yeah, defo, go for it!' So we had these streaks of war paint across our faces when we went down the red carpet and posed for the photographers. I'd probably say no to that now, or at least think twice, as it looked pretty daft.

But the more you are photographed, the more you become aware of it and the kind of image you are putting across. I guess that is why some real A-list celebrities, who have been doing this for years, avoid getting photographed unless everything is completely managed, so that their image is totally controlled (not that I'm in the same category!). I never want to be like that, but as I say, I am more aware of how it can come across, and now avoid anything that might be taken the wrong way.

So, this party was at Battersea Power Station in London and was really good fun. Amy and I couldn't believe we were there, along with all these celebs. We couldn't stop giggling as we met all these people we had loved when we were growing up, like Example, Lethal Bizzle and Professor Green – and, oh my God, they were recognising us!

It was great, and pretty overwhelming. Tinie Tempah was singing that night, and he also recognised us. He asked, 'Can Essex girls sing?' before handing us the mic. Needless to say, after we'd had a go and had given him the mic back, he said that no, we clearly couldn't sing!

All the free drinks and food at the event were a new thing for us, and although I have got used to it now I haven't forgotten how lucky I am to be in this position. There were people walking around with trays of champagne and cocktails and all these random little canapés. It takes a while to get used to controlling yourself at these things – you would leave all of the showbiz parties very drunk and very full otherwise. You get spoilt really, and that's not something I ever want to take for granted.

Same goes for the goody bag that you get given at the end of most events – it is now normal for me to get bags of free gifts and presents everywhere I go, but in the beginning it was a real novelty. Again, I never want to forget how lucky I am, and I make sure I am always really grateful for things like that. I'm always giving stuff to my family and friends, and a lot of it goes to charity.

One thing that makes me laugh, looking back on that night, is how much our families enjoy our fame. I remember mine and Amy's mums at our front doors as they saw us off, wishing us loads of luck for the evening and telling us to have fun. They were really excited for us. But now when we head out, they are like 'Yep, whatever, bye. Don't wake us up when you get in!' It's funny how these kinds of events that are like the best night of your life the first time, soon become almost normal and just part of the job.

There were people walking around with trays of champagne and cocktails

No one has ever actually taught me how to pose for the pictures at these events though – it is just something I have learned myself. I spent a lot of time looking at early pictures to see what looked right and wrong. For example, I used to smile a lot more, as I do think smiling is the best thing in pictures, but I could see that as I have big cheeks, they went up too much when I smiled and I didn't like how it looked. So now I just give a small smile, or I try to smile more with my eyes than my mouth.

I don't like my arms, as I think they are too big. Even when I lose weight, they don't slim down – I know, as I have tried! I think years of doing gymnastics as a child has kind of bulked them up. So I have learned to always, always have one hand on my hip in pictures, which makes my arms look smaller and draws people's attention away from them, as my body is creating a different shape.

Another thing I don't like are my ears. I think they are too big, so you will hardly ever see them in pictures. Even if I have my hair up, I always pull bits over the tops of my ears to hide them, or at least make them look smaller. I hope you are not laughing at me as you read this, cos I know it sounds crazy! But everyone has things they don't like about themselves. And like all these things, it is only by trying stuff out that you know what works for you.

I keep quite close track of what pictures of me appear in the media. My manager, Adam Muddle, watches closely as well, but I still like to get the *Daily Star* and the *Sun* most days, and I look at the *Daily Mail* and the *Mirror* online. I have a Google alert set up for my name as well, so if a story appears about me somewhere, it gets emailed to me. That may sound extreme, but I like to see what is being written, and I like to collect the stories for the memories.

I get most of the weekly celebrity magazines as well, because even when there is no story about me in them, I am still interested in what is being written about people I know. I have got pretty used to being written about, but I still get a bit of a buzz when it is a particularly good article or a picture where I am happy with how I look.

I have a book at home with all my cuttings since the show began – there are hundreds, if not thousands, of articles in there now.

Generally I have been pretty lucky – I haven't taken too much abuse for my appearance in the papers, and I have only once appeared in one of those articles criticising how celebs look – touch wood! It was just a 'hoop of shame' in one of the magazines, and it was for being spotted out with rollers in my hair, which I didn't really mind.

I like to look glamorous, but I am not going to pretend I always look like that, or refuse to leave the house without being completely made-up. I live on a private road with a field opposite, so I am quite lucky in that way – photographers can't really sit around waiting to get a picture of me without being noticed. And if they are there, it is normally because I have tweeted that I am going out or something, in which case, if they do get a picture, I am going to be happier with how I look as I will be prepared.

But if I am just going to the shop, I will put on a trackie and sunglasses and not bother with make-up, and I think that's OK. The only thing I might do is put something on my skin if it is not looking good that day. Having my skin criticised is probably the thing that would upset me the most. But other than that, I think I am quite tough-minded, and criticism wouldn't bother me too much. I'd try not to take notice of it.

The other thing I have done occasionally to make sure the pictures that are printed of me are good is make an agreement with a photographer for paparazzi-type shots. It's always a bit of a weird one, because I don't ever want to set up fake photographs. But on the other hand, if there is something that you know the press want a photograph of, it is sometimes better to have the picture taken in a situation where you have some say and earn some of the money as well.

For example, when I split up with Joey, I got together with a guy called TJ. Due to the growing success of the show, I knew the first pictures of us as a couple would be of interest to the public, and photographers were trying to get it. So if I made a deal with a photographer to have the photos taken, in exchange for some of the money and a chance to check them before they were sent to the press, I could have some control over what went out, and everyone else would be happy too. I don't see that there is any problem with me earning money from photos like that – why should everyone else earn money by printing a picture of me when I don't even get a share?

So, in this case, my manager Adam arranged for a photographer we often work closely with to do the pictures, and gave him a time and place where we would be. Then, as TJ and I walked down the road doing our own thing, he took a series of natural-looking photos that got picked up in the press the next day – job done!

I have also got involved in doing photos like this when, for example, we are doing beach shots. There is nothing worse than being pictured in a bikini at a strange angle, or just as you breathe out, or squint into the sun. So if I know I am going on holiday, I will often arrange with a photographer to be pictured over one afternoon. We make the pictures as natural as possible, and I just do whatever I would be doing normally, but afterwards I look at the photos before they are sent to the press and choose the ones I think are best. This means I can make sure no photos are going out that I don't like – and I can also relax for the rest of the holiday because I know that people won't be taking pictures without me knowing, as the value of any photos will have gone down after the first set have gone to print.

This may seem like a strange thing to people not in the industry, but from the inside it honestly seems to make sense. And I can say that the majority of celebrities are doing set-up pictures. I hear about it happening all the time. For me, the rule is to only do it in situations that are real anyway – I would never do a set-up picture of something that was not actually true in my life. In the end, image is such an important part of any ongoing TV career, and it would be naïve not to try to control it as much as possible.

The one place I do have total control over what photos go out to my fans is Twitter. I have got quite into the website, and I love putting up photos of clothes, or friends, or me doing something, as it is a great way to share stuff. But, like all these things, I have learned along the way by making mistakes!

At my twentieth birthday I tweeted a picture of me and my friends in our knickers but topless after a spray tan. It was a pre-party girls' sleepover, and we had a great evening. I tweeted saying what we were doing and that I couldn't wait for my birthday, and loads of fans replied asking for a picture, so I just put it up. I only had about 50,000 followers at the time, and I don't think I realised the impact it would have. Funny comments from other Twitter users were about all I expected.

But we woke up hungover the next day to see the picture in all the papers. All my friends were like 'Oh my God' but I just had to laugh about it. And I have learned from it – I understand the impact these things can have, so I wouldn't do it again.

That was just me being naïve, but if people with more experience do something like that, it really is just attention seeking, and I would feel very uncomfortable doing something like that now that I know better. It annoys me when people do things just to get photographed. For example, I remember

Lauren Pope grabbing me in the street once and kissing me on the lips in front of photographers as we left an event. I was shocked, but the paps took the photo, and of course it was picked up in the press the next day. I was annoyed by it – that is not the kind of thing I want people to think I need to do to get publicity. Perhaps I am more grounded than some of the cast because I have a close family around me, whereas people like Lauren Goodger and Lucy Meck don't, which is a shame. But I know my own boundaries and what I am happy with and I do my best to stick to that.

As far as interviews go, I have got used to them now as well. And to be honest, most of the journalists are really nice to us. They don't over-analyse the show, but accept it for what it is. Actually I think most of them are fans of it, so we just end up having nice conversations instead of getting grilled about difficult stuff. I think they realise we are probably quite good role models. But it is still weird for me to be asked really personal questions by someone I don't know well or have just met, like things about my family or sex life. But I realise they are just doing their job, and it is part of being famous.

We didn't really get any media training or advice on what to say when we did our first interviews, but there were ITV press officers for *TOWIE* listening in on the chats, I guess to make sure we didn't say anything we shouldn't. I have quite a good head for what to say and what to keep secret though. I was quite clued up from day one about what could be twisted or taken to mean something else, so I never had too many of those kinds of issues. Some of the cast weren't though – and still aren't even now, to be honest. Some people get it, some learn along the way and some people will never quite grasp it.

But, oh my God, the only answer I regretted giving in the early days was about who my celebrity crush was. Every journalist asked that question, and I told them all Plan B and really gushed about him. So it appeared in all their articles, and it sounded like I was a bit obsessed! But I guess it was good I got it out there – and I have since found out that he knows about it … I got to go backstage at one of his concerts, and one of my friends was like 'Oh, Sam fancies you,' and he was like 'Yeah, so I've read.' Very embarrassing! We have seen eachother at several events since then, and always get on well. At the Brit Awards this year, the newspapers implied that we were flirting but really we were just hanging out and having fun. I think we are both too focused on our careers to be looking for a relationship with each other, but he's a lovely guy, so you never know – one day perhaps!

The only answer I regretted giving in the early days was about who my celebrity crush was

I get asked some questions over and over again. The most common one is: 'How has your life changed since the show started?' And I always have pretty much the same answer. I tend to say something along the lines of 'In some respects, massively. I have got fans and people want to take photos of me. But the core things are the same – my friends and my family. I still sit around the table and have dinner with my family, the way I always have done, so in that way life is just as normal as ever.'

I also get asked a lot about why Essex is so much fun, about clubbing and about my beauty routine. But I don't get bored talking about it – it's my life and I love it!

The core things are the same – my friends and my family. In that way life is just as normal as ever

Another common question is 'Is your main thing in life men and money?' I think it is a hard one because really the answer is 'I suppose it is.' But the question is asked in a way that makes it sound as if that's a bad thing. However, think about it – obviously I would like to settle down at some point and, honestly, everyone (not just in Essex) wants to earn money. I think women in Essex are now more ambitious than the men. We want to be powerful, we want to be at the same level as the boys. We want what they have but better – so if a man gets a Range Rover, a girl will get one but with a better spec. And most Essex women, when they set their mind on something, will succeed, trust me. Just wait and see what else I have my mind set on!

My Tips for Red-carpet Posing

- Always put one leg out in front of the other to elongate it. I always go for my right leg.

- Put the opposite hand on your hip, and let the other one hang down by your side. This stops you looking too square, and if you have broad arms it will distract from that. I have my left hand on my hip, with my right arm hanging by my side.

- Breathe in and you will get more definition on your neck, which looks better in a picture.

- Keep your chin up to better define your jawline. Or if you are confident you won't get a double chin, you can always drop your head a little and look upwards for a sexier look.

- It sounds obvious, but smile! It makes you instantly more likeable. Or, if for whatever reason you don't want to smile, at least squint your eyes a bit, so they look smiley and friendly. Don't pout unless you are doing it to be fun – a genuine attempt at pouting doesn't work for 99 per cent of people.

4

THE MEN
IN MY LIFE

Sorry for the bad news, boys, but I am actually already married. The lucky lad is Wayne Marshall. I wore a white puffball dress with beads and a bow as we exchanged vows, and Billie was my maid of honour. We swapped rings while friends and family looked on, and a man called Tom was the vicar. The only problem was, I was only seven years old, and poor Wayne probably didn't know what he was letting himself in for!

Yep, we got married one Saturday afternoon at a friend's house. One of the 'lucky' parents had to pretend to be the vicar, and I wore the dress I had worn as a flower girl for my Aunt Libby's wedding just months before. We had rings, although who knows where they were from – probably a slot machine, or a Christmas cracker. Everyone else pretended to be guests, and after the ceremony we even had a reception. There was no divorce – Wayne and I just grew apart, I guess. I wonder if he even remembers – as a girl, I certainly do.

Finding 'The One' and getting married is something I have always hoped I will do. It's just that so far it hasn't happened. And it's not for a shortage of boyfriends, I will admit!

I am one of those people who definitely spend more time in relationships than out. It's not that I am afraid of being alone – I am independent enough for that – but I enjoy being in a relationship, and I always seem to come across someone at the right time. I throw myself into every relationship properly, and put everything into it – I believe in giving it your full effort. If you don't believe in the relationship, you shouldn't be in it.

Finding 'The One' and getting married is something I have always hoped I will do

That wholehearted determination is something that has always applied to me, even with my first boyfriend. And yes, Wayne, despite my young age, was not even the first!

That honour went to another little boy whose parents were friends with my parents. He was called Billy, and I think I probably tormented him really. I remember always being pretty boisterous with him and grabbing his cheeks whenever I saw him. Our parents used to ask if we were boyfriend and girlfriend, and I'd say yes, while at the same time he would determinedly be saying no! Even in the one picture I have found of the two of us together, it is pretty clear that the feelings were rather one-sided – while I look as pleased as anything as I wrap myself around him, the poor boy just looks unhappy, and pretty terrified. The complications of young love . . . even if I was oblivious to them at the time!

I had a few other boyfriends through primary school – if you can call them that. I remember a guy called Joe who I had a massive crush on in Year 6. My memory is a bit hazy, but I have a feeling he may have been the first guy I kissed. Then there was Harry Lonergan, who was in Year 7. I suppose he was the first person I officially went out with, although a snog and a bit of hand-holding was as far as it went. He was a family friend, and I really fancied him, although now he is more like a brother to me.

Then there was Aaron Corse. Looking back at it, our relationship was so innocent and cute – it was lovely! We used to meet up as part of a group every Saturday. I guess that was the closest thing we got to a date. We were in Year 8, and I remember we didn't kiss for ages, but when we did we were together for six months. He used to do things like pay for my ticket when we all went to the cinema, which I thought was really sweet at the time. But the best present of all that I can remember was when he gave me a £20 phone credit for my mobile. That was amazing, and made me so happy – I only ever bought £5 at a time, so I was really touched!

I guess my first proper boyfriend was Frazer Parrish. Like everyone I had dated up until this point, he was a local guy from a pretty similar background. We got together when I was 15 and he was 17, and we dated for nine months. We first met through friends and started texting each other, and then I saw him at a few house parties – they were the big thing at the time – and I got to know him better. He asked me out, and I remember our first date was at the cinema, but I'm not sure what we saw. Then we pretty quickly got more serious, and he met my parents and that.

He had left school, worked as a builder and drove a car, so I felt really grown-up going out with him. I loved it when he picked me up in his car, even though it was just an Astravan that he used for work – I'd secretly look around to see if anyone noticed me getting in whenever he arrived! His world seemed so far away from mine, as I headed to school in my uniform every day, but I loved that.

He was very generous and gave me some really nice presents. I remember these Timberland boots with fur around the top that I loved, and he also bought me my first diamond. It was a ring with a glass heart with a diamond chip inside it that moved about. It was similar to those amazing Chopard ones, and I still have it today.

Frazer was also the first guy I slept with, and we had been together about three months when it happened. We didn't plan to have sex, but it kind of just happened. We didn't make a big deal of it – I just remember him worrying about me all the time and asking if I was OK, which was nice. I don't regret him being my first at all – I am happy it happened for me while I was in a relationship, rather than the way some people go about it, having sex with someone they don't know well and then wishing they had waited for someone a bit more important. He was a good guy.

That summer my family went to Spain as usual, for the six-week school holiday. Both Billie and I had boyfriends, and they came out to stay with us for a week. But soon after that holiday, my relationship with Frazer just faded. We didn't row, but even though he was older, I think I kind of grew out of him. I was very young when we started dating, and I just lost interest. I say hello if I see him now, but it was years ago – we are both very different people.

The second person I slept with in my life was actually Mark Wright – and this is not something I admit often! But for people who have questioned how far back our history goes, there is your answer. My friend Jerri's boyfriend, Leo, played football with him, and I remember it was in the days before Facebook and Twitter had taken off, and MySpace was the website everyone was using. Jerri and I were looking through Leo's photos on MySpace, and I was like 'Who is that? He's so fit!' about Mark. Then, can you believe, I did that teenage thing of getting her to get her boyfriend to tell him I had said that. I'm not sure what I expected to come of that, and funnily enough nothing did!

I think the first time we actually talked was in Club One9Five in Epping. He knew about me by then, and we started chatting. I was 16 and he was older – I guess around 20 – which at that age can feel like quite a big gap. I didn't know about Lauren Goodger at that time, and he didn't mention her, so I guess they were on one of their off periods, after one of their many rows. Nothing happened for a while – he would just text me every now and then. But I guess that was the start of whatever me and Mark were – or still are.

My friends had started going to a club in Brentwood called Sugar Hut around that time, and I guess I don't have to explain much about that! Even then it was owned by Mick Norcross. We weren't actually old enough to be there at the time, but we pretended we were. I remember going for a night out there once with my sister, Mark and his brother Josh, who Billie was kind of seeing. They were never a couple, but always seemed to be flirting and texting. It was the first time we all went out together.

Then Mark asked me out on the only date we ever went on – until we went skiing on the date that was filmed for series three. How bad is that?! I am sure everyone thought I was exaggerating when I said on the show that he had only taken me on a date once before, but that is totally the truth – Mark is not a date man …

> Mark asked me out on the only date we ever went on. Mark is not a date man …

He took me to Zizzi restaurant in Brentwood High Street, but to be honest it wasn't the best date. I was young and not very worldly, and I didn't know what to talk about. So even though we made an effort while we sat there eating our pasta and pizza, the date was awkward and uncomfortable. We went on to a friend's party afterwards, but it just didn't work out. Mark didn't ask for a follow-up date, and I wasn't really hoping for one.

But a few months later we met at Club One9Five again, and started talking. The chemistry was clearly still there, and we ended up kissing, and later went back to his parents' house, although luckily I didn't bump into them. We went to his bedroom and I slept with him. I don't remember much about it, other than it was quite simple and straightforward – we were too young and inexperienced for it to be anything more!

Nothing came of it anyway – I don't think either of us was up for an actual relationship with the other. And to be honest, I sensed from the kind of texts that he sent that it wasn't going to turn into anything more serious. There was a connection, but that was it. For the time being anyhow.

I still wasn't aware of Lauren, and I am not sure if she was on the scene at that time. I thought he was single, but you never know with Mark. I only found out about Lauren when I started going to Marbella a couple of years later and learned about her there.

But despite the fact that our relationship was going nowhere, Mark and I and our friends socialised together for a while after our one night together, and we had a real laugh. 'There was still a connection, and from time to time things happened, but only after a few drinks, and only really for fun. And then we grew apart again when I got a new boyfriend.

This guy was the first person I really thought I loved. He was called Marc Palmer, and he was a barber. He was older – 22 I think – and we were together for a year. I was really into him, and we had such a good relationship. He really was someone I thought I could have had a future with. He was pretty paranoid though – I remember finding him going through my phone, which was ironic really, because it all fell apart when I found out he had cheated on me with Jodie Marsh. She was just becoming famous at the time, and was pretty well known in the area and on the club scene. Marc didn't tell me what had happened, but she pretty much told the world she had slept with him, so I was hearing it from all my friends. I didn't want to believe it, but everything pointed towards it, so we split up. I was totally heartbroken, and what made it worse was that he would go out with her and they would get papped together. It was so horrible, and so in my face. While everyone else was mad at her for giving Essex a bad name, I was mad at her for breaking my heart.

Jodie is quite notorious as a maneater in Essex – if she wants someone, she really goes after them. She went after Mark Wright – although you won't hear him boasting about that too much!

Mark's reputation as a womaniser is definitely deserved. I can't believe he claims he has only slept with 20 people – I could name 20 women just off my Facebook friends alone. I reckon it is probably triple that, which I guess is still lower than a lot of people would imagine. He is always trying to protect his reputation, and make himself look more clean-cut. But nope, womaniser he is!

Mark's reputation as a womaniser is definitely deserved

Anyway, when I caught Marc cheating on me, I broke up with him and began seeing this lovely guy called TJ. But Marc and I had booked a holiday to Egypt later that year, and I was still young, and to be honest I really wanted to go on the holiday! Despite his cheating, I still had strong feelings for him, and he had been really trying to win me back. So I broke things off with TJ and got back with Marc. Looking back, it was a really stupid thing to do, and I do regret it – TJ was so lovely, as I found out better at a later date!

So Marc and I jetted off to Egypt – and as soon as we got

there I knew I didn't want to be with him. I had grown out of him, and just couldn't get my head around forgiving him for cheating, so the holiday wasn't exactly the romantic getaway of a lifetime that it could have been with the right person, and we split again soon after the holiday.

Sadly Marc was the first but not the last boyfriend to cheat on me. I just don't get it – if you want to be free to be with other people, fine, but don't stay in a relationship! If you are in a relationship, bloody well behave!

I got with my next boyfriend a few months later, when I was 18. He was from Chingford, was very handsome and polite, worked in the City and was just a year older than me. I thought I loved him. We were together for a year, I loved his family and it felt like we were a really good couple. But then he started going off the rails. He was staying out until crazy hours, lost his licence for drink-driving, and then he lost his job. At the same time, everyone was telling me that he was cheating on me, but he denied it and I wanted to believe him.

I remember one night though, when he had a house party and was still out of it in the morning. His phone alarm kept going off and I was trying to wake him, and I went to cancel the alarm. I could see loads of messages on the phone from a girl, and it was obvious that he had asked her out. Normally I am so calm, and when I am upset or angry I just withdraw into myself. But that was the limit for me – I went mad. He woke up and went crazy too – it was the only time he scared me. He pushed me and I fell into the dressing table. He was pinning me down and I had to scream for his brother to come and get him off. It was so weird that he went for me when he was the one cheating – I guess his guilty conscience got the better of him.

Deep down, I knew that the relationship was basically over, but I was having a hard time dealing with my mixed feelings. And then Mark Wright called me. By then I knew he was with Lauren, but we had still stayed friends. He was ringing to tell me Lauren had been cheating on him with my boyfriend. I really didn't know what to believe, but I cut everything off straightaway with my boyfriend, and Mark, who was living with Lauren at the time, kicked her out.

Lauren has always talked on *TOWIE* about us being friends, and how we should all be staying true to the girls, but if what I had heard was true, when faced with a chance to cheat on her boyfriend with another girl's man, she went for it. This is something that I have tried to bring up on the show, but it has always been edited out, and that has really annoyed me. I sometimes come across as the bad guy, 'stealing' Lauren's boyfriend. But the truth is that I only ever did anything with Mark when they weren't together.

I brought it up when we were arguing at Chloe's 30th birthday in series three, but that bit was cut before the show was aired. The producers told me they took it out as they wanted to focus on the cast's present, not our past. I can understand that, but it is still frustrating that I wasn't able to put my point of view across to the viewers.

On one level I feel sorry for Lauren – she has not had an easy childhood from what I can gather, although that is her story to tell, not mine. And despite all her efforts, she never seems to get things quite right. Her outfits and appearance are never quite there, and the way she acts, it's like she has a permanent chip on her shoulder. She is not a girl's girl, and despite what she says, we have never really been friends, and never will be. I wish her well and all that – I just think it is time she stopped pretending to be something she isn't.

Anyway. Back when I was 19, after the split, I was mainly single for the rest of that year – which you may have gathered is pretty rare for me! At this point I went on a lot of girls' holidays to Marbella, and I did go on a few dates, but there was nothing serious. Although I have to say, Mark Wright did keep popping his head up from time to time! But I was never actually dating him.

I went on a few dates with a footballer who played – and still plays – for West Ham United, James Tomkins. He was really nice, but it didn't work out, mainly because our lifestyles were too different. He would be up early in the morning for training, whereas I was a party girl and had late nights all the time, so we weren't going to fit into each other's lives, but I still see him around and think he is a nice guy.

Then I had a holiday romance with a guy called Jorge who I met in Marbella. That was intense and pretty good, and I really did like him. He was just my type, but when we got back home it fizzled out – he lived in south London, and the distance between us just made it too hard. Plus he was very private, and hated the route he thought I was going down when *TOWIE* started, so it seemed it wasn't destined to work out.

And then *TOWIE* really took off. It was probably best for

the show that I went into it single, as it is more interesting for people to watch – but it was good timing, because, as I say, me being single is rare!

TOWIE really took off. It was probably best for the show that I went into it single, as it is more interesting for people to watch

I guess I knew that something would end up happening with Mark again, as he was involved in the show as well. We always had this chemistry, but because we had never tried a relationship, it was like we had unfinished business. I didn't do anything with him when he was dating Lucy in series one, but I was a bit frustrated – because I had introduced the two of them! When we were in Marbella the summer before the show started, I told Mark who she was, and I could tell at the time, knowing what he's like, that he was thinking he wouldn't mind a bit of her!

As for Lauren ... well, as I say, she didn't exactly have a good track record as far as I was concerned, so I didn't feel I owed her a lot. But at the same time I am not a relationship-wrecker, so I never set out to try to cause any upset between her and Mark. I think she did plenty of that on her own! I do find it weird what she put up with though – I think a girl should be made to feel special, and that a boy should be proud to have her on his arm, but he left her at home all the time. She never went to any of his club nights because he wouldn't let her – he wanted to be free to do as he wished when he was there!

After series one, when me and Mark were sort of seeing

each other again, I took him to a Christmas party thrown by my modelling agency, Girl Management. He was there as my guest, but after a couple of hours he disappeared and texted me to say he had gone home sick. I found out the next day that he had gone home with another model – and that just sums him up. He is ultimately selfish – what he wants to do, he does, without thinking how it will impact on anyone else. He wasn't my boyfriend at the time, but it still hurt that he thought it was OK to behave like that.

Not long after that he got with Kayla Collins. I do actually think that was a real relationship, and I know he fancied her, but like so many of Mark's relationships he couldn't keep it going – as there were too many other girls out there to tempt him.

The one time everyone does ask me about is when I told Mark I loved him, after I found out he and Lauren were engaged in series two. It wasn't some-thing I did with the intention of getting him to leave Lauren. It was more something I did for myself, as an attempt at closure, I guess. I thought that if I said it, I would find it easier to move on. I did feel better afterwards and I don't regret doing it. In fact, I think it made it easier to look elsewhere – and that's when I found Joey.

I found out the next day that he'd gone home with another model

I had known Joey for a while before he appeared on *TOWIE*. He was friends with one of my exes, and I had seen him at house parties, and then his cousin began dating my best friend Ferne – see, I told you Essex was incestuous! But I had never really talked to him until we were between series one and two and I went on a night out with Ferne to Revolution in London. We had a proper chat, but he had a girlfriend at the time, and I didn't really fancy him. But he got my number and we began texting a bit.

In the meantime I mentioned him to the producers, because we had been photographed coming out of Revolution, and I just thought he would be good fun on the show. Also the fact that his surname was Essex pretty much meant that he was destined for it! His cousin Chloe had been interviewed for the first series, and although they hadn't used her at the time, I think they had liked her, so it all started falling into place for them.

Meanwhile Joey had split from his girlfriend, so we were both single, and basically he was someone I could have fun and a laugh with, which was something I didn't have in my life at that time. I just really enjoyed being around him, and we grew closer. I don't suppose I ever thought it would last – he is too young, and I was still moving on from Mark – but it was good while it lasted. I think anyone who watched the scenes of us together can see we enjoyed our time together.

Joey had split from his girlfriend, so we were both single

He used to be around my house all the time, and got on really well with my family, which is so important to me in a boyfriend. And yes, I did tell Joey I loved him, and he said the same to me, but looking back I am not sure it was that kind of crazy, deep, romantic love – it was more of a very close friendship.

As for sex, I made Joey wait about five weeks before he got any of that, and then our sex life was just OK. Don't get me wrong, it wasn't bad – he has a great body and he was very sweet – but he just seemed quite inexperienced, and it wasn't amazing. I want more from a man in bed. Give Joey a few years though, and I am sure he will be a real sex god!

Looking back, I can't deny that you do get influenced by the public's opinion. I didn't date him because viewers liked him, but I guess knowing that people liked us together added an extra appeal to him. It's kind of like if your friends like your boyfriend, it can only help. So while our relationship was for real, I'm not sure it would have lasted as long without the show, if you know what I mean.

Anyway, things started to go wrong because we were both so busy all the time. *TOWIE* was becoming more and more popular by the week, and Joey was doing a lot of PAs – nearly every night of the week – and I was spending a lot of time sorting out Minnies. I don't believe in dragging out a relationship that is going wrong, and I didn't want to spend the time we did have together arguing about it – that isn't my thing. And I didn't believe either of us should cut back on what we were doing – at that age your career really does have to come first. So I told him I needed some space, and said that if we missed each other, we could rethink. But to be honest, I found I didn't miss him. There was just too much going on in my life at that time.

Joey was like 'whatever' and was really off with me, and criticised me in the press, which upset me as we had agreed we would not do that. But then we became friends again, and I still think a lot of him. He is a good guy – it is just that I think he is too young for me. I don't want a boy; I need an older man who can challenge me.

I know some people criticised me for not being happy when Joey and Jess kissed after we had split up. It's not that I was jealous, as I had moved on by then, but it was weird, as she was the first person after me I'd seen him snog. But I was also unhappy because she is my friend and I would never kiss a friend's ex. But she'd had a few drinks and decided to go for it, and that was her choice. I decided not to let it break up our friendship, and we discussed it and moved on from it. Things between them ended quickly anyway, and I don't think they would have been suited.

Then I started seeing TJ again – he was the poor guy I dated after Marc cheated on me and then left to go back to Marc. I had always regretted not giving that relationship more of a chance, and then I kept seeing him around the place and we'd have a chat, and then he asked me out and we started seeing each other. He was so lovely, and I felt cared for and happy with him.

Then series three started. I discussed with TJ the possibility of him being on the show, but he didn't want to, and to be honest, I didn't want him to either. I knew what the limelight had done to me and Joey . . .

By now, Mark and Lauren had ended their engagement. My connection with Mark was still there, and we did still flirt – we are weirdly alike on some levels. And Mark kept saying to me, 'We haven't given our relationship a proper chance. Let's just go for it.'

So I cooled things with TJ as the series began, and Mark and I gave it a go. I felt bad about TJ, but I just felt like I needed to know whether Mark and I could have a future once and for all. He is good fun and I love his family – they are so friendly and welcoming. I think Carol is an amazing mum, and we get on really well. I don't have a bad word to say about her. She always takes time to talk to me and we have a laugh. I think she knows I won't be walked over, and admires my morals and business mind. I think she would be happy if I was with Mark.

It's harder with Jess. I think she will always stick up for Mark, no matter what he does, and that quite often puts up a barrier with other girls because of how he behaves. We get round that by just not talking about him. We set all that to one side and just talk as friends. She is older than me by nearly six years, but we can talk on the same level, and I consider her a good friend.

Despite all the plus sides though, Mark is ultimately so self-ish. He will always put Mark first, and I can't see that working for me. It didn't help that he decided to go off to the jungle for *I'm a Celebrity . . . Get Me Out of Here* 2011. Although he asked me to go out to Australia with his family to be there when he got out, I couldn't see that working. I had too much going on in my own career for a start, and I am not the kind of girl who just follows their man about.

Mark will always put Mark first

If he had behaved like more of a gentleman at the time, or been a better boyfriend . . . who knows? But when I told him at the end of series three that I wanted it to end, I meant it. I think he was shocked by that, and his ego didn't like it. He tried to tell the rest of the cast that he had told me to end it, but he definitely didn't – that was what I felt from my heart. I was just glad that we hadn't slept together this time around.

But despite it all, if I am totally honest with myself, there is still something there. There is some mystery to Mark that always pulls me back and means I can never quite close the door on something happening with him again in the future. It's like I can't see there ever being a full stop to me and him, but I just know that now is not the time for that. He will always mean something to me and be an important part of my life.

Once I had realised that Mark and I weren't going to work out, me and TJ started dating again. He really seemed like the whole package. I could trust him and we had a great connection. He is good-looking and generous and he let me believe I was wearing the trousers, even though he could hold his own when it mattered.

But I think we rushed things, and I moved him into my house too early, when we should have taken more time to let things develop. The main problem, I think, was that my lifestyle was too hard for him to take. I am 21 and want to have fun, so I'd go to parties and get pictured chatting with guys. Obviously, nothing ever happened but it was hard for him to see in the papers the next day. Plus he didn't like me filming with my exes, Joey and Mark, and would bring up the past, even though he knew from the start that that was part of my job. It also meant that while each series was on, we hardly got any time together which was hard – and then, when we did, we were arguing.

He was interviewed and filmed by producers for the show, but for whatever reason they decided not to include him – not that TJ minded. He wasn't bothered about being on *TOWIE*, he was just offering to do it for me.

I had started planning a future with him, so I'm sad it ended, but I think he is a lovely guy and hope we always stay in each other's lives in some way.

If I could plan how it would be, I would take a year off from boyfriends. I'd still like to date people, but I don't want anything too deep. I want some time to concentrate on me, my career and earning money. But you just never know when you will meet someone and I certainly wouldn't turn down a guy who could be 'The One' just to fit in with my life plan. And really, if they were the perfect man for me, they wouldn't want to interfere with my plans anyway.

My perfect man would be someone who challenges me. I don't think that any of my exes have really given me a run for my money. Really I want someone who is as ambitious and driven as me, and who has some real life plans and dreams.

I would also want them to adore me! While a lot of my exes fit this description, sometimes they were too soft. They need to hold their own as well! But I do need compliments and someone who will make the tea. And while I don't

My perfect man would be someone who challenges me

want a man who is too flash, who doesn't like to be spoiled now and again?

It would help if they had a nice family too. Spending time with my family and theirs as a group is important to me. My family is everything to me, and I want to find someone with the same values. I think if a guy didn't want children, that would be a real deal-breaker. I have my plan for four kids, and I am sticking to it . . .

In many ways, I'm quite traditional, and I'd be quite happy to organise dinner, and clean and iron his shirts if needed. I think that is the way a lot of women in Essex see things. Having said that, my cooking skills need some working on – I can only just about make a ham and cheese toastie! I blame Mum, as she is so good at all of that, so I have never had to learn.

Where I am not so traditional is that I don't want to be a stay-at-home mum when I have kids. I wouldn't want to be out at work every day, but I'd still want my businesses to be ticking over. And I definitely wouldn't want to stay in every night – I'd still go on dates with my husband – although I don't see why the kids couldn't come along too!

I think that is partly why I am good at socialising with all sorts of people, because Mum and Dad would take me and Billie with them when they went out to dinner in the evening – it was more like a family date. And then we would chat to people, and if we got really tired, we'd just push two chairs together and fall asleep. I think that's a good way to bring up kids. I don't see why parents should completely give up their lives, but at the same time it is a way of not leaving the kids at home with a babysitter all the time.

But who knows if any of this great plan will come true – I know that life can take different turns when you least expect them!

Dating Rules for Men

- It's a rather old-fashioned view, I know, but I think it's great when a guy offers to pay for everything on the first few dates. It shows you're really keen to make a good impression!

- Never discuss exes, apart from briefly touching on them if necessary. No one wants to know their potential new partner's whole dating history.

- Never order food for a girl – I hate that! A girl has her own opinion and tastes, and is perfectly capable of choosing what she wants to eat.

- Dress to impress, regardless of how well off you are. And that means no tracksuits or trainers on a date. You don't need to spend a small fortune on clothes to look like you've made an effort.

- It sounds old-fashioned, but things like opening doors and walking a girl to her front door at the end of the night can earn you all sorts of brownie points!

- Forget game-playing when it comes to who should contact who and when. If the date has gone well, the guy should text the girl to say how much he enjoyed it and set up the next one the morning after. None of this 'leave it three days' rubbish.

- A bit of spoiling goes a long way. You don't have to shower her with gifts all the time, but a perfume, or a lip gloss, or something girly shows you have been thinking of her.

- As for when you first have sex, there is no set rule about that. It should be a mutual decision. Just as long as there have been a good few dates and you feel comfortable with it, go for it!

Dating Venues

Where you take a girl on a first date, and how you behave, are so important if you want to impress! And while you can try to be more adventurous, like Mark Wright, and take a girl skiing or to a cookery lesson, you will have seen on the show that doesn't always work out . . . So if you want to follow a safer, more traditional route, this is how I reckon you should do it.

- The first date is crucial. And no, boys, the cinema does not count! How are you supposed to get to know someone that way? It should be dinner and drinks somewhere with atmosphere, though nothing too romantic. A bit of a dance afterwards would be good too. I can't vouch for other areas of the country, but my favourite venue in Essex for a first date would probably be Sheesh, a Turkish restaurant in Chigwell, because it has a really buzzy atmosphere. And if you are skint, there are cheaper options, like Tarantino in Brentwood, a great Italian place that has a live singer on Fridays. Wherever you live and whatever your budget, do a bit of research before picking your venue.

- For a second date, you can up the stakes a bit. I would like someone to take me into London. I like Little Italy in Soho. They do great Italian food, and have a good dance area.

- Aim for more romance and class for the third date. I like Alec's Restaurant, in the countryside outside Brentwood. It has a pianist, great service and a more romantic vibe. If you get beyond that, just make sure the standard keeps getting higher! And for special occasions, you need to go all out. I like to be taken to the theatre – musicals always go down well with girls. Then go somewhere lovely for dinner and drinks afterwards. If you pick a hotel with a great restaurant and bar, you can book a room there afterwards if things have gone well!

- A few months into a relationship, you could consider taking her on holiday. Somewhere warm and relaxing would be ideal. Dubai would be my perfect location at the moment, and it is close enough to just go for a long weekend if that is all you have time for.

- If you get to the proposal, make it a good one! There is no doubt that this is the guy's job, and it has to be all-out special. It's too personal a matter for me to give any specific advice, but whatever you do, don't propose in public! I don't get why people go down on one knee in a restaurant in front of loads of people. Somewhere private and romantic is a much better idea.

5

LOTS OF LASHES
AND LIP GLOSS

While diamonds are of course amazing, I really feel an Essex girl has two more important best friends: false eyelashes and lip gloss! If there are two things that I would really hate to be seen in public without, it is these. Some girls underestimate the difference they can make to their appearance, but trust me, they are the two basics that make a world of difference to how you look.

Not that I don't like to use plenty of other make-up as well, but I am not someone who will trowel it on – I hate seeing someone who is too made-up. They are doing themselves no favours, as not only is it bad for their skin, but it ends up making them look older. Make-up needs to be applied very well to look good.

I can't really remember when I first started wearing make-up. Looking back at my old school photos, I guess it was about a year after I started at secondary school. My friends and I would spend hours putting it on in the toilets at school, or trying things out on each other at home in the evenings and at the weekends. On Saturdays we would hang around the shops, and spend any pocket money we had saved up on whatever was the latest make-up we wanted to try out. I am not sure if the boys appreciated what we were doing, but we had fun working it out for ourselves anyway.

My friends and I would spend hours putting make-up on in the toilets at school

When I was in Year 10 and Billie was in Year 11, we moved to Spain for five months and went to an English international school out there. It was a weird experience for us. Don't get me wrong, we loved Spain – the weather, the lifestyle and the place were great , and we learned some Spanish and met different people. But ultimately it wasn't for us – Billie and I missed our home and our friends, so Mum made the decision to move us back home, even though Mum and Dad were really happy out there. Looking back, I suppose we were quite selfish about it, but we were young and didn't realise it at the time. Laude Lady Elizabeth Senior School was a good school though. It was a mixed-sex private day school in Lliber in Alicante, and had great facilities, like a huge swimming pool, games courts and loads of new computers and that.

But one massive difference I noticed between that school and our school back home was their attitude to make-up. The teachers would stand outside the assembly hall with make-up-remover wipes, and they would make you take off any make-up you were wearing as you went in. Try doing that in an Essex school – you would have no chance! Literally, one little bit of bronzer and they would make you take it off. No girl in an Essex school would stand for being told to do that . . .

Looking back, on the one hand, I can see why they did it, but on the other hand, you are at an age when you are experimenting and starting to fancy boys, so it is only natural. Also, if you suffer from acne, a bit of foundation can actually make all the difference, not only to how you look, but to your confidence.

My nan always used to tell me I would laugh at myself in the future, and true enough, looking back at photos from those days, I guess I do. But who cares – at the time I thought I looked hot!

And to be honest, Billie and I definitely looked better than a lot of our classmates, because we had one of the best make-up teachers to learn from – our mum's younger sister, Libby, was a make-up artist as we were growing up. I remember her doing make-up for celebrities like Blazing Squad, and some-times we were allowed to go and watch her at work. So I think we picked up some tips from that.

The only thing that bothers me about make-up on young girls is how soon they start putting on foundation. Unless, as I said, you have problem skin in the first place, it is the one thing that will actually create a problem. Young skin should really be allowed to breathe – so save the foundation until you are older and need it. I see all these young girls coming into Minnies with it totally caked on, and it really annoys me, as their skin is so fresh and young, yet they are clogging it up. I'd definitely steer girls away from the foundation for as long as possible.

Instead it should be all about bronzer and highlighter on cheeks. Bronzer gives you a nice glow that makes you look like you have been in the sun. You can brush it all over your face, especially on the places where you tend to catch the sun the most. Then use highlighter on your cheekbones to add a shimmer and draw attention to them.

But the all-important thing for an Essex girl is false eyelashes – they are a must. Big, thick, long lashes look really sexy and glamorous, and you can never really get that look without using false lashes, no matter how great your own eyelashes and mascara are.

False eyelashes – they are a must!

You will never see any of the girls on *TOWIE* without their lashes, even when they are just relaxing at home. In fact you will never see them make-up free at all, but lashes are the most crucial.

I started wearing them when I was about 16 or 17 and was beginning to go out clubbing. Back then, I saw them as something glamorous and to be saved for a special night out, but slowly they became more and more an everyday thing, and now you will rarely see me without them. Occasionally they can be a pain – like if you forget to take them off after a late night and you wake up with your eyes stuck together, or one set of lashes on your pillow, but generally I couldn't do without them. I wear one pair of lashes if I am having a casual day, but when I go on a night out, I normally wear two pairs, to get a really thick, dramatic look. I have tried out a few brands over the years, but at the moment my favourite is Eylure. Their lashes are numbered, and my favourite are the 107 and 140 sets.

For me though, false eyelashes are especially important because I suffer from a condition called trichotillomania, which means I pull my eyelashes out – that sounds weird, I know! So although not many people know it, I don't actually have any lashes at all. Sometimes little short ones will appear as they start to grow back, but I will just pull them out again before they have a chance to grow. It is hard to explain why I pull them out. It is like a habit that I have, so I do it without thinking. I do it when I am nervous, or bored, or even when I am asleep. I don't even realise I am doing it.

It started when I was about eight or nine. Someone – I can't remember who – said to me that if you find a stray eyelash and blow the lash away and make a wish, it will come true. And I think I decided that the more I did that, the more chance my wish had of coming true. I don't even know what I was wishing for, but I guess it was something I wanted really badly, because I was doing it a lot, and then it became a habit. Before I knew it, I was doing it without thinking, and that is when I started doing it in my sleep too.

My mum saw what I was doing, but didn't really under-stand why, and wasn't sure how to stop me. She'd get pretty frustrated with me, but I carried on doing it, so in the end she took me to the doctor. I can't really remember what they said, but it didn't work, whatever it was. Another time, I went to a hypnotherapist. That worked for a bit and all my eyelashes started to grow back, but then I started doing it again.

I was really self-conscious about my lack of lashes when I was at school. I went to Raphael Junior School in Hornchurch, which was an independent school – and is actually where I became good friends with Amy Childs. Our mums have been friends for years, so we grew up playing together.

The kids there were taught to be really polite and well behaved, but people are still nosy, and little kids tend to just ask any questions that come into their heads, don't they? So when they realised I had no lashes, they would ask me about it. I was embarrassed to tell them the truth – and it was so hard to explain anyway – so I would always make something up.

My sister Billie was really good to me about it, and would help me make up stories to stop people from asking me about it all the time. I remember one time she told me to say I had done a handstand against the wall and then I'd fallen over and all my eyelashes had fallen out. How crazy is that? It shows how a kid's mind works, because I am sure it made sense to the pair of us at the time. Who knows, maybe the other little kids believed it!

Once I got to secondary school, I discovered eyeliner, so things weren't so bad. I learned to smudge a bit around my eyes, and then people didn't notice my lack of lashes so much. That made me more relaxed about it, and I was able to just tell people the truth if they asked me.

Now I feel I have kind of come to terms with it. If anything, it annoys my mum more than me now. I probably will try to overcome the problem eventually, but I don't feel as though I have the time for it at the moment. I still don't normally talk to people about it though. It's just those close to me that know about it – up until now of course! My family and boyfriends all say I look beautiful either way – but I guess they have to! I can see that other people are surprised the first time they see me without my lashes or make-up on.

I have actually done two shoots for magazines where I was supposed to be make-up free. They were articles to show that despite being on a TV show where appearance is so important, we are just like anyone else without the make-up. People wanted to see what we looked like once the make-up was stripped away, but I couldn't quite bring myself to do the shoot with no lashes. So on one shoot, I wore a little bit of eyeliner smudged in, and on the other, I wore a really thin pair of false lashes. They were so thin though, they were still smaller than most people's own lashes – and definitely a lot smaller than Amy's, who was doing the same shoot! I hope no one thinks that was cheating. I felt so exposed, there was no way I'd have done the shoots otherwise.

Luckily my eyelashes are the only hair on my body I pull out – other people with trichotillomania pull out hair from all over their bodies so, for example, they might have no eyebrows. But while my eyebrows are naturally thin, they are all mine! My eyebrows are quite fair, but annoyingly they are not the shape I want them to be, so I have changed them quite a bit.

I think I waxed them for the first time around Year 11. I tried eyebrow tattooing once, but I didn't like it. It was too painful to get done, actually quite stressful, and I didn't even think they looked good. They were too dark and prominent, and on me the colour didn't hold well and faded quickly. I think they look too obvious – I prefer them to be more subtle.

I get HD brows now. It is the most fashionable way to do them, and for a reason – it works really well. The beautician uses a mix of techniques to get you the right brows, so they do things like threading, waxing, tinting and tweezing. It is so much better and despite all the work that goes into them they are actually quite natural looking.

I need my eyebrows to be quite thin and well shaped because of the shape of my eyes. I love my eyes – they are one of my favourite features about myself. Everyone always says they are very cat-like, and I think they are unique. Over the last year I have used a lot of make-up artists, and they always say they love working on my eyes, as you can do a lot with them. They can carry off most styles and types of make-up and I try to make them the focus of my face.

I like to have smokey eyes, and use a lot of light- and dark-brown eye shadow colours blended together, although I generally avoid black, as it is a bit too dark and heavy on my eyes. I also like using a lot of gold, which is great for my eyes – if you have green eyes like me, it always looks good, as it really complements them. It's important that you learn which colours work best for you, to go with both your eye colour and skin tone.

Having my make-up done by other people was something I got used to when I was modelling. I already had a reasonable idea of how to go about things, as Aunt Libby had taught me and Billie a few good basics, but it was the artists on those early modelling shoots who I learned the most from.

Whoever organises the shoot will normally arrange for a make-up artist to come along too, and before anything else is done, they will do your make-up to go with the theme of the shoot. I would watch closely in the mirror and ask them to explain things, then I would buy the products and brushes that I thought worked best and copy their techniques myself at home.

The two main things I learned during those shoots were blending and the importance of brushes, both of which I think people forget about. Blending the right colours together, and really making it look like one flows into the other, is so important for a good look. But equally, so are the brushes you use. They need to be of a good quality – trust me, you can see the difference when someone has used a low-quality, cheap brush. And you need at least one different brush for everything. I will use four different brushes just to put on my foundation.

Now that I have done so many shoots and learned so much about make-up and techniques, sometimes it is hard for me to keep my opinion to myself – if I disagree with what the make-up artist is doing, I really have to bite my tongue and put my trust in them. Generally though they are pretty good and talk it through with you. And occasionally, if I am given the choice, I will opt to do my own make-up, because I am so confident in it now.

On the actual show, we all do our own make-up. Everyone is surprised by that, but it is our real lives, so it wouldn't make sense if we had make-up artists coming to our houses and making us look different from how we usually do. Having said that, all us girls will get people in before big events such as awards ceremonies to help us out.

I reckon the person who does her make-up best out of the cast is Billie, because like me she has spent a lot of time working out what works best for her. But I also think Maria does a really good job. She spends a lot of time on her skin and foundation, and gets it pretty perfect – her skin looks so even sometimes, it is like she is a mannequin!

I reckon I spend about £75 a month on make-up, and my favourite brand is MAC. I am quite a loyal customer, and go to their Bluewater store all the time to stock up. As a perk of being well known, I have a loyalty card that gets me 20 per cent off. I find that weird though – that the more famous you get, and the more money you have, the more perks you get. It's like things are the wrong way around – not that I'm complaining!

I get sent a lot of free make-up now too. Sometimes it comes in goody bags at events, sometimes it is given to me when I do signings, but a lot of the time it is sent to my management. I am really appreciative and thankful for it, but obviously I can't use it all, and it is not all appropriate for me. I have quite sensitive eyes, so I need to be careful when it comes to eye make-up in particular. But of course I never throw any of it away, and a lot of it goes to friends and family. I also have a huge drawer full of products for when I want a change. It's great fun digging through it.

The one make-up item I can never have too much of is lip gloss. Never underestimate the power of the lip gloss! I am addicted to it, nearly as much as I am my lashes. When I put it on I instantly feel happier with myself, and sexier. I don't know whether it's the way it reflects light or what, but my lips look instantly bigger and better – and it's the same for everyone. I don't know anyone who doesn't look better with a touch of lip gloss, whether it is tinted or clear.

Never underestimate the power of lip gloss

My favourite is MAC's Dazzleglass Lip Gloss. Sometimes I just wear it on its own, but if I want to make more of an impact, I will wear lipstick as well. I like to experiment with colours – I wore dark-purple recently, and I have coral and nude shades too, but really I prefer them in matte-red and dark-red. And I will always use a lip pencil too – mostly MAC Spice Lip Liner. It makes quite an impact.

I haven't always worn these products though. At school everyone was obsessed with Nivea's Pearly Shine, which came in a candy-pink colour and made your lips all shimmery. It only cost a couple of quid, and everyone had it. I think they still sell it today. Now, however, it's all about the gloss.

No matter how much I love my make-up, I make sure I take it off at night. Or at least, I try to most of the time – sometimes, after a heavy night, I admit, it may have to wait until the next morning! But generally I will take it off before bed and put Nivea moisturiser on all over my face and body, so I can wake up fresh the next morning and put all the make-up on again!

How to Get the Perfect Lashes

- There are many different types of lashes, so make sure you find the one that's right for you. I love the Eylure range, especially 107 and 140, but try different ones out, and decide whether you just want a few subtle extra lashes, natural-style, or a full-on look that lets the world know you are wearing them!

- Cut them to size. There is nothing worse than a false eyelash strip hanging off the end of someone's eyelid because they haven't trimmed it down.

- If you want to keep using the same pair of lashes over again, you will want to put mascara on your own lashes first. If you are not too fussed about keeping your falsies in perfect condition, you can put it on after they are attached. This creates a more natural look, but does mean that they are not as easy to reuse.

- Put eyelash glue in a thin line along the lashes – I tend to use the one that comes with the Eylure sets – and wait 30 seconds for it to dry a bit. It is easier to stick it on when the glue is a bit tacky, rather than still runny. It also means you won't get any of the glue showing.

- Then stick them onto your eyelids, as close to your actual line of lashes as you can, lining them up from the outside of your eyes, and pressing firmly once they are in place.

- When the glue has dried, put eyeliner over the top of the eyelash join to really blend the join into your eyelid. And you are all ready to go!

- Get it done professionally the first time if you are unsure – MAC make-up counters do makeovers for a fee, and really show you how to do a good job of it.

What Is Trichotillomania?

Trichotillomania is a compulsive urge that makes a person pull out their own hair. It can be triggered by stress or depression, or it can happen subconsciously. I do it when I am asleep, or not thinking about it, but some people do it when they feel tense, and pulling the hair out relieves that. The most common place to pull hair from is your scalp, eyelashes (like me) or eyebrows, but people also pull hair from anywhere else on their body really. It can be treated with the help of therapy, or some people can just grow out of it.

You can get more information and support at www.trichotillomania.co.uk

6

LIVING THE DREAM?

Like everything in life, being famous has a good and a bad side.

Don't get me wrong, I am not complaining about the bad bits – there is nothing more annoying than a famous person, who's living a great life and enjoying all the perks, having a good whinge about how tough things are for them, just because of a few less than amazing things they have to deal with. That really gets my back up, so I promise this chapter won't be like that ...

Like everything in life, being famous has a good side and a bad side

And to be honest, I thought there would be a lot more negatives to being in the public eye than there have been. I was actually prepared for a lot more, but really the press and the public have been good to me and the rest of the *TOWIE* crew the majority of the time.

For a lot of famous people, one of the big problems is who

you can trust. When a family member or friend gets offered big money to sell photos or stories, it can often prove to be too tempting. But luckily I can happily say this has not happened to me so far.

Billie and I share our friends, and our friendship group is the same now as it was before *TOWIE*. It is the same bunch of girls we have sleepovers with, go out partying with, and share our secrets with. That is how I like it, and I want it to stay that way. Our friends think it is funny when we go out and we get people coming over wanting a photograph or a chat, but they are fine with it, and just roll their eyes and laugh. They know we haven't changed, so they treat us exactly the same as they always have, and I know I can trust them. Occasionally the odd person who I haven't spoken to for years will get in touch, but I don't really fall for that – I'm just polite, and then get on with my life.

Touch wood, I also trust my ex-boyfriends not to sell stories as, while things might not have worked out for us, I think they are all decent blokes really. Anyway, even if they did, I don't think there is anything for me to be embarrassed about. I can be quite a prude, so nobody has naked pictures of me on their phones to sell to the papers or anything like that!

As for the people in Brentwood, local businesses are loving the show. Business is booming because of the attention *TOWIE* has brought to the town, and a lot of them have had renovations and other work done. If anything, the only bad thing is that sometimes there are so many tourists around now, especially at night, that the locals occasionally say they can feel a bit pushed out – like when their local pubs become crowded. But I guess there are always two sides to these changes.

Most people in Essex are really friendly to me. All the young girls and their parents that I bump into around the place on a day-to-day basis love the show, and will stop to give me advice on what I should be doing next, or who I should be dating. Sometimes older women in their thirties and forties, who didn't get the chance to do what we are doing when they were younger, will make comments about our dresses, or look at us like we are dirt in a club. But I take no notice of that.

I also do a lot of PAs – public appearances – where businesses such as shops and nightclubs pay me to come and spend time at their venue. I usually have to pose for photos, or sign autographs for fans, or be interviewed on stage – whatever they think is of interest to their customers. This can be well paid – I can earn several thousand pounds just for an hour or two of work. Pretty nice!

PAs can be quite exhausting because they are all over the country, and when I do nightclub appearances I don't arrive at the venue until midnight or later. I try to take some friends and make a night of it, staying on for a few drinks and a dance, but sometimes – if it is last-minute, or late on a work night, or really far away from Essex – and I can't rope any of my friends in, I end up going on my own.

Although generally people are positive, it can be quite daunting sometimes, and you never know how people will react to you, especially when you go to student nights and people have had quite a lot to drink. This is the main reason why I have a tour manager who comes along with me. He is called Ian and he works for a company called Peace of Mind Services, which is pretty much what he gives me! He is partly my driver, to get me to the venue on time and give me a chance to sleep on the way back, but he also does my security for me. He is a big, muscly guy, so not many people give me hassle when he is around, and it is reassuring to have him there.

I remember once being at a PA with Harry in a bar in Bristol. It was a vile place – the floor was sticky, I was scared to even set my bag on the sofa and it was full of hillbillies – you know the kind of place! Harry was on stage doing a Q and A, and this group of lads was yelling over the top of him. Poor Harry was trying to talk, but all you could hear was them going 'Who are ya?' over and over again. I got really annoyed, so I stormed on, grabbed the mic and said, 'Don't be jel, be reem!' and everyone else started cheering. I always think people who react like that are just jealous people who want a bit of our lives. And true enough, afterwards when we were doing photos, the boys queued up to get their pictures taken with us.

People are generally positive though, and we only get this kind of negativity at about one in ten PAs. You just deal with it. Often it is just people who have had a lot to drink and get rowdy or over-friendly, trying to hug me all the time. But that is what Ian is there for. Ian doesn't come along when I have a normal night out with friends though, and sometimes I wish he did.

Check out the chubby cheeks on me! Even at three I was loving the sunshine in the garden in Spain.

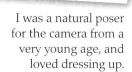

I was a natural poser for the camera from a very young age, and loved dressing up.

Billie and me were always doing one routine or another, and in such cool PJs too, don't you think?!

Mum and I have always been close. She puts me and Billie first – we are a great family!

Of all the places we chose to pose for a photo in Year 7, we chose the toilets . . .

Me and Lucy hitting the shops on one of our many Saturday shopping trips.

Me and Lucy loved the photo booth in the Post Office on Brentwood High Street when we were 12.

Messing around in the school playground – Billie's friends and mine got on well even in high school.

On a school trip to Norfolk when we were 13, clearly thinking we were cool!

Amy and Billie at Billie's eighteenth birthday party round at our house.

Camping at V Festival in Chelmsford – before *TOWIE* days, so no VIP! Check out Billie, third from left, with her red hair!

Amy, Harry and me in our retro gear at a 60s party that was filmed for series one.

Me and the girls enjoying the sun – and the partying – over the May bank holiday in Marbs, 2010.

Me and my little Harry messing around behind the scenes. I'm always going to think of him as a little brother.

Me and Joey in happier times, on a romantic holiday to Majorca.

We were on Alan Carr's *Chatty Man*. It was great fun, though he got us drunk on Lambrini!

Me and Amy soaking up the sun in Marbella, 2011. We didn't know there were paps around, honest . . .

Lydia and me were doing facials behind the scenes on *The Essexercise Workout* DVD.

This was the day Minnies opened to the public for the first time. Nervous and excited!

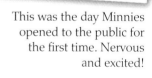

So close: Billie, Mum and me at my twenty-first birthday party.

On the red (or blue) carpet at the British Comedy Awards in 2011, where we presented an award.

I felt like a million dollars in my Anoushka G dress at the National TV Awards, 2012.

Me, Amy, Lauren and Lydia hit the red carpet at the BAFTAs 2011 – one of the best nights of my life!

I was so excited to meet Rihanna. She is one of my idols, and was so lovely and stunning in real life.

We had a horrible night during series three, when a gang of people attacked me and Billie, leaving me in hospital. It was covered a lot in the papers at the time, and really shocked both of us. It made us so conscious of the downsides of being well known.

A gang of girls attacked me and Billie, leaving me in hospital

We were at a club called Jet Black in London and a group of girls started on Billie. There was an argument, then one girl hit me, and I instinctively lashed back at her. Luckily the bouncers saw the incident and threw them out.

In all the pushing though, Billie got dragged out with them, and the argument continued. Billie was punched in the face and ended up with a split lip. It was so shocking. We found out later that this bit of the attack was filmed on someone's phone, and it went on YouTube the next day. Poor Billie watched it back a couple of times, and got upset all over again. But in a way it was good it was filmed, as it was proof of what they had done, and showed just how shocking their behaviour was.

Later that night, I was attacked by the same group of people. My friend Charlotte called an ambulance and I was rushed to hospital. My eyes apparently rolled back in my head, and my brain had swollen because of the beating. I needed a brain scan, and was covered in bruises and scratches. I had two black eyes and had lost a lot of hair.

I was in agony for a week or two after, and was so upset. I just sat at home and cried, and tried to work out why it had

103

happened. I think these girls were motivated by jealousy of our fame and how successful we were because of the show. I don't think they would have behaved like that if we had just been ordinary girls on a night out. In a way it was good that Billie and I went through it together, as we could talk about it and relate to each other.

It still makes me angry thinking about it now, that a group of girls could do that to another person. They were like a pack of animals, and that is scary. For a while we debated taking security around with us all the time, but that just seems so extreme. I want to be able to live a normal life, without worrying that bad things could happen anywhere I go. So in the end we decided to just learn from it, and avoid any clubs where we might not feel safe, but other than that, we would use our security just for events we were hired to attend.

Billie and I reported the gang to the police, and they took our statements and photographed our injuries. The case is still open pending enquiries as I write this at the beginning of 2012.

It was such a horrible experience, and was reported in newspapers and magazines, even making the cover of a lot of them. The upside of what happened was the response we got. It was amazing how many people cared – from our true friends, to fans who put notes of support through our doors, to people we had worked with in the past who sent huge bunches of flowers. There was also huge online support too – the number of my Twitter followers went up by 45,000 in the few days following the attack. How crazy is that? I am sure some of them were just being morbidly curious, but I think most people were genuinely concerned, and I got so many amazing tweets.

I have had to develop a thick skin when it comes to Twitter, I have to say. Don't get me wrong – like PAs, the majority of it is positive. I'd say that for every negative tweet, I get 50 positive ones, and generally people message me about my outfits, or to ask for advice, or to give me support, but sometimes people can be really nasty and small-minded.

I took a lot of abuse for dumping Joey. You'd think I'd committed mass murder or something, judging by some of the comments! At first it really upset me and I started to doubt whether I'd done the right thing, but then I realised that I have put myself out there to be judged because of the show, and I need to see the bigger picture. Most people have dumped someone, so it's really not that they thought what I had done was so terrible. They just wanted to get a rise out of me. Things like that don't bother me so much now – I just block the people who make nasty comments! One thing fame has taught me is to become more thick-skinned.

Despite all this though, the worst thing for me by a mile that has come about because of my fame has not been the physical or verbal attacks, but the coverage about my family. On that front, two stories appeared in the press that I wish more than anything had not.

One was about Dave Chatwood, who has looked after me and Billie since I was two, and in every way other than biologically is my true dad. I can't go into detail about things here, but the fact is that Dave has been the most amazing dad. He has always treated us exactly as if we were his biological kids, and his priority has always been to look after Mum and Billie and me, always trying to give us the best.

The other difficult story involving my family that I have had to deal with was about my biological father, Lee, and claimed that he had attacked his girlfriend, Fay Simmons, in June 2011 and had been convicted of assault. For me, what Lee did was really bad. Beating up a woman is just horrible and you can never justify it.

Mum grew up in Hornchurch in Essex, and married Lee when she was 20 and he was a few years older. From what she has told me, he was very handsome, in a kind of tanned, almost gypsy-like way. He was full of energy and fun, into activities like water skiing, and he lived on a farm where he rode horses. He was wild and loved living life on the edge, which I guess Mum was really attracted to. I like bad boys as well, so I can see where she was coming from!

I'm not sure what caused things to go wrong, but from what Mum has said, it sounds like Lee was really jealous. Apparently he would just go mad, like he would go off on one at her about her friends, as though his jealousy had taken over. When Billie was around one and I was a baby, and Mum took us to the shop ... well, you aren't going to get around Tesco quickly are you? But after an hour and a half, she would get home and Lee would be going mad. He would hit and kick Mum, once so badly he broke her coccyx bone – the one at the bottom of your back. She had to go to hospital and pretend she'd had a water-skiing accident. Other times he would half strangle or suffocate her, and the police would be called by worried neighbours. He would never go for me and Billie on purpose, but one time Mum was holding me and he threw a spanner at her. Apparently it missed my head by about a centimetre. He was just clearly a violent nasty piece of work.

Mum is a very strong woman, and she was worried about him being a danger to us, but part of her still loved him, and she kept thinking he would get help. My granddad, Chris, Mum's dad, who lives in Brentwood, worked out what was happening, and he stepped in and convinced her to leave. It was a big family drama, but everyone was there to support Mum and she knew

My mum is a very strong woman

she needed to get us all away from him. I know she asks herself now why she didn't leave sooner – she has always told me and Billie, 'If a man hits you even once, you leave. No second chances.'

Mum got divorced from Lee, and while she had no contact with him herself, she didn't try to stop us from seeing him, so his mum, Nanny Wendy, would take us for visits. Nanny Wendy is amazing. She really tried to make sure we kept up a relationship with our dad, and to be honest, a lot of the time we would go and see him just for her. She called me and Billie her 'Miss Worlds' and has always treated us so well. Her relationship with us is really strong – she has also remained close to Mum – and she flew in from Spain for my 21st birthday party last year. We love Nanny Wendy!

Billie and I haven't really had contact with Lee for years now though. As far as I am concerned, he was violent to our mum, so I don't want to know him, and I will never forgive him for what he did. It is a shame things didn't work out for him in a family sense, but ultimately I am not interested. That is probably horrible for him to hear, but really he chose to do what he did.

Don't get me wrong, I want him to be happy in life, and I think he has some good qualities – he can be funny – but I don't need to see him. Dave is our dad; Lee failed as our dad. He never helped Mum financially or emotionally. Dad did that.

Lee has gone on to have three more kids by three different women, so Billie and I have two half-brothers called Beau and Harry and a half-sister called Ruby. I do have a bit of contact with them, but they are not really part of our lives. I hope that one day, when we aren't so busy, we can be more involved with them.

What upsets me about Lee though is that he didn't learn from his early mistakes. Of course, it makes me sad, and it is hard that my relationship with him is now out there for every-one to read about, but like everything in life, it has just made me tougher and more able to tackle life in general.

Anyway, enough about the negatives … and on with the positives!

7

WHITE STILETTOS?
AS IF!

Essex fashion is amazing. You won't find anyone else who puts in the effort and thought that Essex girls do, and you definitely won't find anyone who looks better. We have had a lot of grief over the years for our fashion sense, but I reckon that is just coming from people who are jel of the Essex look, or who have no fashion sense themselves. The idea that we totter around in white stilettos and short dresses and have no sense of taste or class is out of order, and just plain wrong.

We have definitely developed our own sense of style. We like things to be bigger, bolder and better. We also like to take a fashion and go for it 100 per cent. No half measures for us! We like to make an effort, and are happy for people to realise we have. What's the point in trying to do things so subtly that people don't even think you have tried? What a waste of time!

Obviously fashion is ever changing, but there are two rules to getting it right Essex-style, that always work. Firstly, clothes must be classy, sexy and glam. Secondly, remember that high heels usually look best. Of course there is a time and a place for pumps or Ugg boots, but these are the rules when you are going on a night out, or are really aiming to look your best. Then it is all about the heels – and the higher the better. No compromises! And no, I don't mean white stilettos – unless they go with the outfit obviously!

I have always been really into fashion, even when I was a little girl. Wearing something that makes me look and feel good has always been well important to me, and I have always loved trying out new colours and styles.

When I was really young, I was a real girly girl. My mum would dress me up in little dresses and skirts, and I'd walk around feeling like a little princess. I also loved fancy dress – my favourite was Snow White, although I also wanted to look like anyone who was on the Nickelodeon channel at the time. Everyone from the Olsen twins to Sabrina the Teenage Witch were like my fashion icons. I also had a long gypsy skirt that I thought looked like it was one of Mary Poppins' – hardly a fashion icon, was she, but I loved it.

When I was really young, I was a real girly girl

My favourite shop was Tammy Girl. I loved all the glitz and the glitter – it seems all you have to do to make a little girl want certain clothes is make them sparkly!

Looking back, Tammy Girl was pretty tacky really, but we loved all the matching outfits, and I remember that fashion for wearing skirts over trousers. Whenever Billie and I were going to a party at someone's house when we were at primary school, Mum would be like 'OK, girls, time to visit Tammy Girl' and we'd be so excited. Even then we thought fashion and clothes-shopping was amazing.

I remember once we had a fancy-dress day at school – I guess I was about six or seven at the time – where you had to come as a music idol. Billie was Cher, Amy Childs was one of the girls from Abba, and for some reason Mum decided it would be a good idea for me to go as Dolly Parton. I wore a wig, my face was all powdered and made-up, and I had fake boobs made out of tissue stuffed under my vest top. Oh my God, I swear I looked like I had walked straight off one of those American beauty pageants. It was so funny, and I loved it – I remember that day clearly, even though I was so young. All the boys were like 'Sam has boobs!' and suddenly they all wanted to claim I was their girlfriend. It was an early taste of how lads are, I guess – even at that age! It's funny though, how things have changed – if a mum sent their kid to school like that now, they'd probably be told off for it, but back then it all seemed so innocent. I had great fun!

Mum has always been a cool dresser, although she has quite a different style to me. She goes for a smart-casual look, and looks her best in a nice pair of skinny jeans with heels.

But I think my casual stage, when I was around ten, was too much even for her. I went through a kind of chavvy, trackie-wearing stage, and I'd always be in trackie bottoms and my Nike Athletic jumper. It was the fashion at the time – think Sporty Spice, that's the kind of look we were going for. But Mum hated it, and tried to get me out of it. Luckily for her, that stage only lasted about six months. Even though it was fashionable at the time, it's one of the few outfits I look back on and say to myself, 'What were you thinking?'

Sporty Spice wasn't my favourite Spice Girl anyhow – that was Geri Halliwell. When I was nine I wanted to be Ginger Spice, and even got a copy of her Union Jack dress. We used to dress up as the Spice Girls, and I would be Geri, Billie was always Baby Spice, although she never wanted to be, and two of our friends were Posh Spice and Sporty Spice. We couldn't find anyone to be Scary Spice though, so we got hold of this girl who lived nearby and was just six, put dark bronzer all over her, backcombed her hair and told her she had to play the part. We looked so stupid, but it was great fun. We never got tired of dressing as the Spice Girls.

Around this time, I was obsessed with these clown necklaces from Argos. I don't know if you remember them, but they were gold or silver clowns on chains, and everyone wanted one. It was the most random necklace. Mum finally caved in and I got one – but only in silver, not in gold. Looking back, they were proper chavvy! I also wanted a sovereign necklace, which I wasn't allowed. I did get one of those half-and-half necklaces though, where you give one half to your friend – Sarah Fahy, who was my best mate at school, had the other half of mine.

Sarah and I used to have a right laugh and do mad things together. I remember we once spent a whole day trying to make a video to send in to *You've Been Framed*. We tried pushing each other off a trampoline, one of us walking in on the other shaving her legs in the shower, and falling down the stairs. We never actually sent in one of the videos though, so all we achieved was a load of bruises!

By the time I went on to senior school, I was pretty confident in myself and my fashion choices. I took real pride in what I wore, and yeah, I'd say I was quite a trendsetter. I remember turning up on my first day at school in my navy skirt, knee-high socks, little jeans jacket and Pringle bag, with my hair in bunches. I was rocking a Britney Spears kind of look. I am sure some people were like 'Who is this new girl, and what is she wearing?' But before you knew it, all my new group of friends were doing the same.

By now my favourite shop was H&M. I was allowed to go shopping in Chelmsford with my friends from Year 8 onwards – and we went every week. Mum would drop us at Brentwood station on a Saturday at 11 a.m. and pick us up again at 5.30 p.m. The boys came too – it was almost like a big group date – and they would just kind of hang out as the girls went round the shops. We never bought too much, just a couple of things, maybe a nice cardigan or something. At the time I loved wearing jeans with pumps and cardies. As well as H&M, I liked the jumpers in Gap, and then New Look started coming onto our radar too. Topshop was a bit pricey then, and wasn't as big for teenagers as it is today.

Mum would give us money for the train and food, but I always had £20 of my own to spend on clothes, which I earned from my first real job – working on a farm. Each Saturday morning, from eight till ten, I would go to a farm owned by a family friend. It wasn't a working farm – I think the woman just loved animals – and she paid me to feed them. So I had to feed horses, cats, peacocks, dogs, even turtles! Twenty quid was amazing for two hours' work at that time, so I was well happy with it. I think I did better in terms of pay than most of my friends. The boys mainly got their money from paper rounds. After we had been shopping, we would go to the cinema, and they would pay for the girls' tickets with the money they had earned.

Sometimes we went somewhere other than Chelmsford, although we weren't allowed into central London until we were older. We went to Romford for a bit, but it was rougher and there was rivalry with our area, so Mum would ring our mobiles all the time to check on us. In the end, we decided it wasn't very nice, and swapped back to hanging out in Chelmsford.

We were getting into going out at night now as well, and I have been up for partying ever since. So that means spending a lot of time in the afternoons and evenings getting ready. I put a lot of effort into my make-up and hair, as you can tell from other chapters, but it is choosing the outfit that really takes the longest. I throw clothes everywhere, especially when I am getting frustrated – some nights my room looks like a battlefield! The chaos is still there in the morning to deal with, but Mum doesn't let it remain like that for long. She gets on my case the minute I wake up. Not good when I have a hangover!

The most expensive item of clothing I own is my school prom dress that I wore when I was 16. It was handmade in Amsterdam and is a gold mermaid-style dress with beads sewn all over it. It is very Beyoncé, very glam, and very me!

It cost £600 and was a present from Mum and Dad. I was properly touched at the time – I think that must be the most they have ever spent on me in one go. I've still got it now, and am dying for an excuse to wear it again. It is something I will always keep, and I hope I can pass it on to my daughters one day too. It's well nice to have these classic pieces of clothing that you can keep and get out from time to time, and then pass on through your family.

I know some people will hate me for saying this, but I would love a fur coat for that reason. I love animals, and if I think about it too much I don't like the idea of furs, but they are such a classic thing to own. I'd love to have a collection of them in my wardrobe one day, even if I never wear them.

But a lot of my wardrobe is taken up by fancy dress. My obsession with it didn't stop when I was little, and I will still wear it whenever I can now, although it is always a sexier version than it was back in the day! So I will still dress up as Snow White these days – but now it is a sexy Snow White, with stockings and a short rather than long dress. Honestly, I have been everything from the Queen of Hearts, to a whoopee cushion. Yep, a whoopee cushion ... I got the outfit from a fancy-dress shop for a party, and even got Joey to try it on. It was brilliant – he looked so funny in it! In fact he might have to bribe me to stop me putting the photo of him in it in this book! Billie hates all that though, so I always have to bully her into joining me in wearing silly outfits. Getting her on board for the Halloween party you saw in series three of *TOWIE*, for example, was not easy. But she looks great when she does it, so I won't give up on her just yet.

Of course my taste in fashion has changed since being on the show, for several reasons. Watching myself on screen and seeing photos of myself means I've been able to take a more objective view of what suits me. Also I obviously have more money to spend on fashion. And once I was getting out of Essex a bit more, I was seeing alternative ways to do things. Don't get me wrong, I still think Essex girls have the best fashion sense, but I also realised that occasionally less can be more, so I have tried to tone down my tan and my make-up, and sometimes I cover up a bit more than perhaps I did before.

We don't have any help with fashion on the show at all. We are encouraged to just wear what we would normally go for, although all the cast will think about it that bit more, knowing we are on TV. We all have much more choice now when it comes to fashion. After the show had been on for about a month, we, or our managers, started approaching clothing ranges. Apparently it is completely normal for celebs to do that, although it was new to me at the time.

We don't have any help with fashion on the show at all

Now, to be honest, I get so many free clothes sent to me that I haven't any hope of wearing them all – not that I'm complaining!

The idea is that the brand hopes you will be pictured or filmed in one of their outfits, and this will then increase the sales. I remember high-street brands like Siren and Hed Kandi were especially keen for us to wear their clothes and accessories, even in the early days.

So, if you look back, you'll see that while we've all more or less kept our Essex sense of style, it was rather more typical in series one, if you know what I mean. I remember I had on a short, white, low-cut bodycon dress with a lot of cleavage on show when we filmed the opening credits. I had worn the dress before and liked it, and when I brought along a range of possible clothes to wear, the producers liked it too, as it is very Essex. But I'd probably avoid that now, as it is a bit revealing and not as classy as I prefer now.

For the Christmas special after series one, I upped my game and went for show-stopping outfits, and I think that's when people started noticing my style. Then the next month, January 2011, at the National Television Awards, it was my first outing where I really felt like a million dollars, and the coverage of the event was really positive about my dress.

My favourite though was the dress I wore to the BAFTAs in May 2011. I borrowed a white and black Diane von Furstenberg wrap dress worth £3,500, and I really felt like an A-lister on the red carpet. It was the first time I had borrowed a really expensive outfit to wear to an event, and I couldn't believe this amazing designer was happy to lend me the dress and thought I was a good representation of the brand. I had thought that kind of privilege was reserved for the likes of Angelina Jolie and Jennifer Lopez! But in reality it seems all the celebrities are doing it, which is lucky, because I would never be able to afford those kinds of dresses, especially with so many events to go to over a year. I don't suppose the A-listers ever have to actually fork out for an outfit, which must be amazing.

I did my own hair and make-up that night though, so it

wasn't all A-list glam! Joey was with me and looked reem in Louboutin shoes and a suit – we got so many compliments. Lauren Goodger, in a sequined dress, and Lydia, in a flowery one, both looked great. I felt like it was a proper turning point which made people realise that I had a great sense of fashion. I can definitely say that night was the best I have ever felt in my life, appearance-wise.

I kept up the same aim of classy, sophisticated fashion, but without turning my back on Essex glam, with my outfit for the *Transformers 3* premiere in June 2011. I borrowed a red Alexander McQueen dress, and again did my own hair and make-up, which, even if I do say so myself, looked pretty good in the pictures. Some coverage even said I gave the main star, Rosie Huntington-Whiteley, a run for her money, which was amazing, cos she is gorgeous! A magazine sold the dress I wore for charity afterwards.

Then there was the flowing white silk dress I wore to the ITV summer party in July that year, designed by Halston Heritage. It was the same dress Sarah Jessica Parker had worn in *Sex and the City: The Movie*, which some of the press realised, so I just expected to be slagged off, to be honest. I wasn't intending to compete with such an established fashionista! But I didn't get criticised, and in fact the way I accessorised it was complimented, which was well good.

But even though I love that I can now wear designer dresses to these kinds of events, most of the time I still keep to my high-street fashion. It is what I am most comfortable in on a day-to-day basis, and I like to keep in touch with the fashions that the people who come into Minnies prefer.

I also like magazines that cover high-street fashion rather than high-end, so I will buy *More* and *Look*. I save mags like *Vogue* for the hairdresser's, and I don't end up buying anything in them – I just like to create an imaginary wish list in my head!

When I'm shopping for myself, away from Minnies, I really like Zara, although I go for their brighter, more interesting designs. That bit of bling, the sparkles and the dazzle, are my favourite things about fashion, and I'd never go for anything which lacked that. I love people like JLo and Beyoncé's fashion – in fact I think they are really Essex girls at heart! Or someone like Blake Lively – her wardrobe is so classy, but it's also fun. I want to always be glam! You will never catch me going for a plain look, like I think Alexa Chung does, for example. I don't get her style at all. It's just not me.

I don't always have the time to put in maximum effort though. My life is so busy that I don't have hours and hours to put together an outfit, or perfect my hair and make-up. Some celebs actually have a strict schedule for beauty and fashion. Take Amy Childs, for example. She is much more of a home girl than me, so she will always have the time to blow-dry her hair perfectly before she goes out. But nowadays I prefer to use any spare time I have on my shop, so that would be impossible.

I'm obvioiusly not like lots of the A-list celebs, like Victoria Beckham or Cheryl Cole, who have a whole team of stylists to help them out. I decide on my outfits for myself. The most help I get is from my friend Cafer Mehmet – who we all call Jeff – who works in fashion. He comes round to my house sometimes and gives me and Billie advice on what he thinks looks good, or he'll come shopping with me. He also calls in the odd piece of clothing from someone he knows for me to wear.

But no matter how much I love the glam thing when I go out, you can't beat a good casual outfit when you are on downtime. Obviously it is not always practical to be in a dress and heels, and it also means I can really enjoy going all out when I do! I love being in my Diesel jeans, Ugg boots and leather jacket. Or, even better, just relaxing at home in my onesie! I think boys love that too – that side of a girl when they are relaxed at home in their PJs, with no make-up. It is when they can see you for who you really are, and I think it is appealing for them.

I'm also all for comfort over appearance when it comes to underwear – unless you are dressing for a boy obviously. If you could see under my clothes most days, you'd be shocked! Most of my underwear doesn't match, and I go for wired, smooth T-shirt bras rather than the lacy ones. I hate thongs, so I always go for knickers, and the more girly the better. I have ones with Mr Men on, Batman, flowers, Snoopy … and you name a Disney character, I have a pair with them on. I work with the idea that it's what's on show that counts!

As for shoes, I am hooked on this website called StylistPick. All their shoes are £39.95 when you are registered, and they have some good designer brands and loads of modern styles. They have teamed up with top stylists, who come up with the choices.

I do think a good pair of shoes is really important, as is a good handbag – and I like expensive bags. A designer bag has always been my weakness – I can look at handbags for hours, especially Mulberry's, and I have my one permanently stuck to my arm.

When I was at school though, it was all about the Pringle bag – all my friends had one. But I remember Mum had a lovely Burberry rucksack, and I borrowed it one day and took it to school. I was so proud of it, but then we had break, and while everyone was queuing for the tuck shop and fighting to get served first, this boy pulled on the bag and broke the strap in his desperation to get to the front. I went mad; I had steam coming out of my ears! I started crying and demanded he pay for a new one, but he just laughed and he never did pay for a replacement. It still makes me mad, thinking about that!

As far as other accessories go, I admit, I am really bad. Scarves, belts, hats, sunglasses . . . I tend to forget about them when I'm putting together an outfit. Or, if I do remember, I feel a bit silly – I'd love to be able to pull off hats, but I always feel a bit stupid in them.

The ultimate Essex accessory though is a Rolex watch. Absolutely everyone who is anyone has one. I borrowed mine from one of my dad's friends for a bit, and I liked it so much I decided to treat myself and bought it from him. My first watch was an Armani one with a black face that Mum and Dad gave me when I was 13. Billie was given the same one in silver.

The ultimate Essex accessory is a Rolex watch

Billie loves her bling – the more glitz and sparkle, the

happier she is. I like jewellery that is real though; costume jewellery irritates me. I wear diamond studs in my ears all the time, and I still wear the diamond ring Joey gave me. There is no emotional attachment to it any more, before you read anything into that, I just really like it. I'd never buy myself jewellery though – I think it should always be a gift.

How to Dress if You Look Like Me

- I've got a curvy hourglass figure, so it's important to wear clothes that work for that. There is no point wearing something just because it's in fashion – you have to think about whether it will suit you. I love things that show off my curves, like a pencil skirt or a fitted wrap dress.

- I am very conscious of my thighs, which will never be thin, so while I'll still wear little dresses, you will rarely catch me in anything too short or bum-skimming – it would do me no favours and I would just feel uncomfortable. I prefer to go for glam knee-length or long styles.

- I love my boobs, but there is a limit to how much I'll show off – an overflowing cleavage is never a good look. I hold my hands up, I have been guilty of this

➡

plenty of times, but I've regretted it when I've seen the pictures! Not going for very short dresses helps here though, as it means I am not breaking that all-important rule – never show too much cleavage and leg at the same time.

- I don't like the tops of my arms, so I'll opt for a cap shoulder or three-quarter-length sleeve if I can – flimsy, strappy dresses do me no favours. My shoulders are quite broad, and combine that with boobs and strapless dresses are a nightmare. They make me look huge, so without exception they are a no-go.

- As for colours, I love wearing creams and really rich colours. Creams are timeless and classy, but the downside is obviously keeping them clean. I also love blues and turquoise. Wishy-washy colours like lilac don't go with my blonde hair, and nor do a lot of pink shades – unless I want to look like a Barbie doll.

8

MY BUSINESS MIND

I am not the brainiest person on the planet, but I have always prided myself on being business-minded.

Don't get me wrong, I wasn't bottom of the class at school or anything, but nor was I a brain box. I was probably hovering around the middle most of the time. I wasn't massive on studying, but I got away with it, and was just pretty average.

I did love school, but it was more about the social aspects for me – the friends and the fun. Having said that, I was good at sport and art, and I liked science.

I'm not the brainiest person on the planet, but I have always prided myself on being business-minded

But doing A-levels was never going to be an option for me. Billie had decided to stay on and do them, but I couldn't wait to leave and go to work. I was ready to get out into the real world and earn money as soon as I hit 16.

I think I was partly influenced by my boyfriend at the time, Frazer, who I mentioned earlier. He was 18 and had a car, and I loved the independence he had. As soon as I was old enough, I made sure I passed my test, and I got the money together to buy myself my first car – a Mini. That's how I have always been. If I want something, I will work hard, save up, and make it happen.

That way of thinking has always seemed pretty obvious to me. Money isn't everything, but it makes things happen for you, and I realised that from a young age. We did have money as kids, but it wasn't just handed to us to do what we liked with; we had to explain why we needed it. We weren't spoilt – it was probably like £10–15 at a time – and as soon as we were old enough to have Saturday jobs, we earned a lot of our own pocket money. Other than the farm job which I mentioned in the last chapter, I worked behind the reception in my Aunt Libby's beauty salon in Billericay for a bit. We also did chores for our parents if we wanted more. I would get a couple of quid at a time from Mum for doing the ironing, which I guess was the job she hated most!

My first real job though was when I left school at 16. Looking back, I am really proud of myself – no one pushed me to do so, but I went out and got myself a job almost straight-away. It was at Connexions, an agency that helps young people with the basics in life, such as education, housing and money. My role was basically inputting data, but it was actu-ally quite good fun. I had to ring everyone around my age in the area who had left school and find out if they had jobs, or if they wanted help with courses or apprenticeships. I felt really grown up doing it, and I ended up speaking to a lot of people from my own school and hearing all sorts of stories. That job taught me never to judge a book by its cover. These girls would be coming in with prams, and at first I expected them to just moan and ask for money. But then I realised that most of them were really nice, clever girls, and just wanted to provide for their kids. I was there six months and I feel that I learned a lot from the place – it provides a really important service.

Never judge a book by its cover

But although I loved it, I didn't earn enough, as far as I was concerned. So I started applying for other jobs, got an interview at Lloyds TSB Bank, and was offered a job as customer assistant. I think Connexions were sorry to see me go, as I had been a proper hard worker – that is the Essex girl way, to work hard!

That job was fine, but it wasn't my long-term plan. Not that I had worked out exactly what that plan was, before *TOWIE* came along! I think if I hadn't got on the show, I would probably have worked my way up through the bank and would hopefully be working somewhere in the City by now.

But luckily *TOWIE* came up, and all the opportunities that came with it, and I have been sure to take advantage of as many of them as I can, as I know what a once-in-a-lifetime opportunity it is. I have loved being on the show, and realise that it has opened up so many doors for all the cast – then

TOWIE came up – I know what a once-in-a-lifetime opportunity it is

it is down to each of us how much advantage we take of that.

Minnies Boutique came about after series one. People were constantly asking where I got my outfits from, and my family and I began to wonder if instead of promoting other people's brands, there was a way to create our own brand. Then I would always be wearing clothes I loved, and I could also turn the interest in my fashion to my advantage financially.

We had already discussed as a family how we wanted to open a joint business one day, although initially we thought it might be tea rooms or a posh café, because my family are really good cooks. Well, maybe not me, but my mum and nan are! But then we came up with the idea of opening our own boutique,

We came up with the idea of opening our own boutique

so we approached the *TOWIE* producers and asked them what they thought about the idea and whether they would film it. And actually they loved the idea, and thought it would be an interesting new location to film in.

The four directors of the shop are me, Billie, our mum and my Aunt Libby, Mum's younger sister. She had just sold her house and put forward most of the money we needed to start the business, and I added what I had, and then we got on with finding the venue. We were looking for premises on Brentwood High Street at first, but the rates were really high for a start-up business. Also Brentwood is pretty busy at night, and we were worried about drunk people coming out of the bars and clubs and doing damage to the shop. Sadly I knew that my and Billie's celebrity status could make the venue more of a target for people who had had a few drinks and wanted to show off, and we didn't want to see our new business smashed up.

Mark Wright had been involved in opening a bar called Deuces that had been firebombed just before we came up with our plan for Minnies, and people have asked if we were worried about the same thing happening to Minnies, but we weren't. There aren't the same issues with a shop as there can be with a bar, so we didn't think it would be a problem in that way, but we still thought that a spot just off the high street would be better, so it was perfect when this venue in Ropers Yard came up. We instantly liked it, with the little cobbled street leading down to it, and a car park right next to it, which would make things easier for customers. It just felt right, so we decided we should go for it.

The name Minnies came from my nickname as a kid. My dad and granddad still call me that today. I got the name for two reasons – partly because I used to have a squeaky voice like Minnie Mouse when I was a kid, and partly because I was obsessed with her. I had all the toys and a pair of ears that I used to wear all the time. We went to Disneyland one year and I

The name Minnies came from my nickname as a kid

was so happy when I met Minnie – Mum still teases me about that. It is so weird when you are a kid how you really think these characters are real, and when you meet them at Disneyland you totally believe you are meeting the actual character, not just someone dressed up as them. Oh for the days when life was simple, ha!

So anyway, with a venue and a name, we got on with working out how the hell you actually source stock and run a shop. None of us had any experience before, beyond loving fashion. So we started the whole thing totally from scratch. Libby had worked in bookkeeping before, so she is good at making sure the accounts are in order. Mum is . . . well, she has a touch of OCD, so she keeps the shop itself in order! There is never a thing out of place on the shop floor when Mum is around! She also does the merchandising, which means making sure the clothes are displayed in the best way, that we have the right amount of each item of clothing ordered, that pricing is correct, and so on – all the stuff that sounds basic, but can make a huge difference to the appearance of the shop and to sales.

My Aunt Sam – my mum's older sister – also works with us in the shop. She isn't a director, but she does a lot for us, like handling the shop's blog, the PR and our Twitter account. She used to work as a radio plugger for a lot of the big music acts, and has had a great life travelling around the world, so she is good on the promotional side of things – like getting the shop coverage in the media and organising launch parties. So that left me and Billie to actually source the clothes – exactly the role we wanted to have! But we admit, we were starting out with very little knowledge other than our own fashion sense, and we weren't too sure how to put that into practice.

My friend Jeff, who I mentioned before and who works in the fashion industry, knew people to introduce us to and places to take us. So through that, we worked out quite quickly how to make things happen for us, and pretty rapidly we were at home in our roles.

The only problem was, we did not exactly have long to open the shop. We figured the producers would be happy to film us building up to opening the shop throughout series two, with the actual opening right at the end. But no. They told us they wanted to show viewers the opening party in the first episode of the series. Hello?! We had found the venue in February and the series started in March! So it was heads down everyone, and we did the fittings, stocked it – although admittedly only with four brands, whereas now we have loads – and opened it as requested. Phew!

You might remember the opening party on the show. It all looked relaxed on screen – apart from when Lydia's pig Mr Darcy, peed on the floor of course – but the reality behind the scenes was a lot more stressful. We didn't even have enough stock in on time, so we had the clothes really spread out, to try to make the shop look full. Other than that, I think it went fairly smoothly. Obviously we didn't get everything totally right first go, as we had opened so fast, but it was the right thing to do really.

And to be honest, the shop was closed a lot in March, as we were doing so much filming, and otherwise we'd never get to have a conversation without a customer interrupting. I guess that is an example of the compromises you have to make when filming a reality show. Usually there are hundreds of people in and out of Minnies every day, so while we try to keep as close to reality as possible when filming, sometimes the door really does have to be closed to the general public for practical reasons.

There are hundreds of people in and out of Minnies every day

So the opening on the show was like a soft launch, and then we did a proper big opening in April, when the show was over. It was manic as soon as we unlocked the door. That day we had 3,000 people queuing along the little cobbled street. Can you imagine that? It was exciting, but also worrying – what if no one had liked our clothes? But everyone was great, and we got really positive feedback. All the cast popped in – except Lauren Goodger of course – to wish us luck and check out the place, which was lovely of them.

At the end of the day we had made £8,000 of sales, and every day for those first few weeks we took between £3,000 and £5,000, which is absolutely incredible for a boutique, as anyone in retail can tell you. A lot of places won't even take that in a month. We were so happy. I've never been so proud as I was on that first day. We went to celebrate in a little terrace bar nearby – just close friends and family and people who work in the shop.

Since then, Minnies has just kept growing and growing. We have all put so much into it, and have made a real effort to learn everything we can about the business.

So much of it is about knowing your customer. In the beginning it was all young girls coming in, fans of the show, who had saved up their pocket money or wages to spend in the shop. They generally spend no more than £30–60 a visit, so at first there was no point stocking high-end designer clothes. I remember that first month we were selling mostly value-for-money jumpers, dresses and floral shirts – the simple, inexpensive stuff was just flying off the shelves.

Now we also get older, richer clients, so we have expanded our range to include more expensive brands. We even get the odd grandmother popping in, although I am not sure if they are buying for themselves or their grandkids. My glamorous nan, Liz, always pops in for a few things for herself when she is in the area, which I think is great. She must be our oldest customer!

As far as whether people are coming in because they like the shop or because they are *TOWIE* fans, I would honestly say about 70 per cent of our clients are there because of the show, and that is not something I have a problem with – I know the show has been a huge reason for the shop's success, and I'm happy and grateful for that. Fans come in because they want to see me and Billie, and then they will often look for something to take away as a souvenir. I do think the shop would have done well regardless though – there are not many shops like it on Brentwood High Street, and it is per-fect for the local market.

I know the show has been a huge reason for the shop being successful

It is the hen parties that make me laugh most. These groups of girls will come from Cardiff or wherever and book in to a hotel in Brentwood, and then they will basically do their own *TOWIE* tour. They get straight off the train and come to

Minnies to buy an outfit to wear that night. So they will turn up with their little cases in tow and pile into the shop. Then that night they are off to Sugar Hut. Not being big-headed, but they want to see me and Billie in the shop, or Kirk and Mick in the club, so if we are working it can properly make their weekend.

When we are filming the show, we are not often in Minnies, but in the months in between, Billie and I make a real effort to be there as much as possible. It is our business after all. We will be there serving on the shop floor at least three or four days a week, particularly at weekends, as we know that is when most tourists come to the area to check it out because of *TOWIE*. Some days I think I spend more time standing around having my picture taken than serving! But it's great, and I really enjoy it. Seriously, I never dreamed two years ago, as I headed off for another day behind the counter in the bank, that this was how I would be earning a living. It's amazing!

Profit-wise, people say it takes a year on average to earn back what you put into the business when you set up a shop. We did that within about two weeks – not bad, eh? But we haven't been taking big wages – so far we have put most of the money back into Minnies, so we can improve and expand. The hard work is far from over.

Once the store was up and running, the next big project for us was to get it online. Fans of the show from around the UK had been in touch asking how they could buy clothes without having to travel to Brentwood, so it seemed the obvious thing to do. But, wow, we hadn't realised just how big a project it would be. It was more work than setting up the shop in the first place!

We decided to aim high from the start, so we began with about 400 items for sale online, which was a huge task. Each item needed to be photographed on a model and we had to write a full description. And you can't just say 'plain white T-shirt' or whatever, you have to give details of the material, any detailing on it, how to wash it, and so on. And then we needed to work out how many of each item we needed to stock, which was quite hard to get an idea of at the start, as we didn't know exactly what response we would get. We decided that Billie and I would model most of the clothes, with a couple of models to help us out. So we did a shoot with all the items, which was fun but exhausting.

Opening up this side of the business also meant that we needed more staff. We have an internet team now, who deal with getting everything online, checking the orders, merchandising and customer services. We also use an outside distributor, so we pass the orders on to them, and they deal with the actual sending out of the clothes. With this extra staff, we now have seven people working for us as well as the four directors. It's mad when you look at it like that – I'm 21 and a director of a business, with a team of staff working for me. I never expected it, but I love it!

Not everything went smoothly with the online part of the business though. We held a party for the website and all my friends and family came down to Sugar Hut to celebrate the launch, which was supposed to be the next day – but then it didn't happen! There were a few technical glitches, and

Billie and I weren't completely happy with the look of the site, so we decided it was better that it went up late, rather than on time but with mistakes. I'm glad we waited, as we didn't want to launch a site that was just OK – and actually, the delay worked to our advantage, as it built up people's interest.

Eventually though it went live on 7 October 2011, and within the first ten minutes, it had 410,000 hits, which is insane. It was so popular that the server went down and people were struggling to actually place their orders.

We could see all the people online buying from our end, which was a great feeling. People were still on the website buying at 3 a.m!

It was funny, because the stuff modelled by me and Billie sold the quickest. The most popular was a little brown fur gilet and skirt that I modelled, and a blue jumper with a heart on it that Billie modelled. Also massively popular was a pug hoodie we had given Amy Childs, and which she had worn on *Celebrity Big Brother* the month before the site was launched. She wore it loads in the house, and I think that really helped sales of it. We sold 300 of those alone on the first day.

The website is ten times harder than running the shop though. It is just on such a huge scale, and it takes constant work. We update the online range every two weeks, which means doing fresh shoots and writing descriptions all the time. But I get a real buzz from it all, and would never complain.

We have been very lucky to receive help from a few pretty high-profile businessmen who have seen how well the website is doing, but realise we are new to it, so have offered up advice when we need it, with no strings attached. On an average week now, between the shop and the website, we take about £40k of payments, which is amazing.

One of the highlights for me since opening Minnies was when we introduced Beyoncé's range, House of Dereon. As I am always saying, I am a massive fan of her style, so when I heard that she was bringing out a range that stayed true to the kind of fashion she goes for herself, I was really excited. I was like 'Billie, we need this in Minnies now!'

One of the highlights since opening was when we introduced Beyoncé's range

To make it even more exciting, one of the perks of getting her range into the shop was that we got to go to the fashion show that launched it in Selfridges in London – and she was there! It was well good to see her in person – she is stunning – and there was a great vibe to the event. I felt really privileged to be there with all these proper fashion people.

The other big step we then took in our business was to bring out our own range. Until then, all the clothes we had stocked in the shop had been other people's designs and lines, but we had always intended to create our own when we got a chance, although there was so much going on at the time that we didn't think the opportunity would come so soon.

Basically one of the ranges that had sold the best in Minnies is called Maggie + Me, and House of Fraser also stocks their range. They saw a massive increase in its sales in their stores, and couldn't believe the impact the show was having on it. So they contacted our friend Jeff and asked him to chat with us about the possibility of doing our own stuff.

We decided to go for it, and in between filming – yep, trust me, it was madness! – we put together a range of 35 pieces that we took to House of Fraser. They were really positive about them, and ended up buying 31 of the styles and stocking them in-store! It was so exciting. I remember being at Meadowhall in Sheffield for a signing before the range launched, and being shown the area in House of Fraser where they were going to have the clothes. It was mad – it's such a huge store, and only two years before even having the money to shop in there was a big deal for us, so to have our range stocked there was like a dream.

We decided to call the range GraciEve, after our cousins Grace, who was nine at the time, and Eva, who was seven, who are Auntie Sam's daughters. We had brainstormed what our typical customer would want, and went for real Essex girl glam, glitzy and dressy, with diamantes and sequins.

Outside designers came up with the outfits, but we chose what we thought would be right for our range and bought them in. In the future though, I want to be able to actually design the outfits myself from scratch. I want to sit and sketch out how I envisage an outfit to be, although I am not a good drawer at all, so I guess I'm going to have to work on that! But I have so many designs and visions in my head. I would love to do catwalk-style outfits but at high-street prices. Really creative, flowy dresses with bits cut out and trouser suits. Pieces that look stylish and expensive, but are affordable for everyone.

But for that first GraciEve range, we used other designers. It was insane though – we put our entire budget into the clothing, and suddenly realised we had none left for the labels and packaging! So just a few weeks before it was due to launch, our house basically turned into a factory. We had our friends around, and everyone was pinning labels into the clothing and packing them up. It was a madhouse, but it was the only way we could get around it, with no budget left to pay someone else to do it!

For two weeks I remember poor Mum getting in from Minnies at like 11.30 p.m., and then working on GraciEve at home, while I would be off doing PAs around the country, and then go home to do the same. But it had to be done before Christmas – and in amongst all of this we had to do the advertising shoot.

The range was exclusive to Minnies and House of Fraser, and the deal was to keep it like that for two seasons, before opening it out to other stores. Right from day one though, we already had shops asking about stocking it, which was so exciting – it meant people really believed in us. Some days I really have to pinch myself, as it has all happened so quickly. Sometimes I will have moments of doubt, and think it can't be real that all these people suddenly want clothes chosen by me. Then I realise it is reality, and if I don't concentrate and get back to work, it will all fall apart!

As a family, our dreams for our businesses have no limit. Now our plans are to just keep expanding. We want more Minnies stores around the country – it would be great to have one in the North, and one in the Midlands – and, who knows, we might even go abroad. We have had interest from Dubai – how amazing would that be? Of course I am sure it would be crucial for me to go out there a lot to get that set up!

The business side of things is really important to me, because much as I love *TOWIE* and the celebrity stuff, I have no idea how long it will last – that will be largely decided by the public. But what I can do is take responsibility for how well the businesses do.

I would like to be comfortable by the time I am 30, as I don't always want to work. I want a large family, and I want to be a mum who has time to be at home with my kids. I don't want to be like Jordan, still doing the business and celeb thing at the same time as raising a family.

Don't get me wrong, you can't really knock Jordan for that, because she is clearly a great mum with happy kids, and she is also a great businesswoman. I'm not sure about her choice of men though, and the way she puts her family in the lime-light, but that is the way she has done it, and it's her choice. But I don't want to be like that.

And I definitely don't want to be posing in a bikini or leo-tard when I've had a few kids! It's a free country, and everyone has their way of doing things and all that, but I'd rather look smart in a dress and jacket or something – an outfit that gives off the right signal and a genuine image of who I am.

For now though, I am really happy with where I am at, and if the businesses continue as they are, there is no reason I won't achieve my aim. As for the other *TOWIE* cast members who have businesses, fair play to them – we all know the show won't last forever, so it makes sense to open up other options for yourself. But I hope people always remember that although people have opened up other shops since the show began, Minnies was the original!

Kirk already had Sugar Hut, Mark already did club nights, and Peri's family already had the card shop, all of which have increased their success off the back of the show. But we were the first to think of the potential the show could bring to a new business.

I think the next was Jess and her underwear shop, With Love Jessica, which is lovely, and there isn't really anything else like it in the area. She thought of the idea after she had her boobs done and couldn't find good bras. It's a hard market to tackle though, because for everyday underwear, a lot of people – if they are like me – go for comfort over looks. Jess's underwear is more about the latter, and they are very expensive for everyday wear.

Also if you are going for some all-out underwear, or if a boy is looking to buy a girl something special, you go for the more established brands, like Agent Provocateur for example, don't you? So I am not sure she is going to smash it and get lots of bestsellers. And, to be honest, Jess's heart isn't really in it – her passion is singing. That is what she cares about, so I think she should put all her efforts into getting her singing career to take off. Maybe her mum, Carol, or her little sister, when she's older, should take over. Or even Nanny Pat!

I think the next business that came about was Lauren Goodger's tan, Lauren's Way. Well, I guess someone had to bring one out, didn't they? And if it was anyone, it should be her – she always has quite a tan on her these days! If I'd been asked to do it, I'd have said no – I wouldn't want to be forever associated with fake tan. I'm not even sure that it's Lauren's own business – I think maybe she just put her name to a brand. From what I know of her, she isn't very business-minded, and she doesn't seem that passionate about it to me. But it's done well as a brand, so I wish her success and all that. I can't tell you what it is like though, as I have never tried it! Despite all the free clothes she has had from Minnies, I have not been sent one free bottle of the tan, which doesn't impress me! I did feel sorry for her when she tried to open a shop for her tanning range, though, and it was firebombed hours later. As with Mark's club, it was probably the work of jealous people, but that's why you have to be so careful. Good on her for not letting it put her off, and for reopening it.

Then there is Lydia's vintage store, Bella Sorella. I love her shop, and it is good to have a place like that in Loughton. It is so Lydia! It really reflects her style, which is so different to the usual Essex look – Lydia is unique! But I do worry that her clothes won't do so well – because I think maybe the locals like to look at them but not actually buy them. But I think the furnishings and cakes and frames are adorable, and they are doing really well. I also love that she loves her shop. When we are on shoots or filming, she will be in the corner on her iPad, checking on new stock and ordering new brands. She is like me and Billie – it is something she is genuinely enthusiastic about.

So at the moment I have income coming in through the shop and a steady income through my *Star* magazine column and various other interview fees. Then I also earn money from appearances. These can be the personal appearances in clubs that I mentioned before, or shop openings or launches of products I have agreed to back. When I am there, I usually just have to pose for official photos and do a meet and greet with fans, but I have been asked to do more random things as well, such as read a bedtime story to shoppers, or pull pints of gravy for passers-by! I am normally paid a few thousand pounds for an appearance, and will be there for a couple of hours, although it can mean travelling quite a bit, as I will do this all over the country. I enjoy doing PAs, as it is a great feeling to meet all the fans, the people who have made *TOWIE* what it is.

On my way to a recent event where I was getting £8,000 for a two-hour appearance, I was thinking about how crazy it was. That was a very high fee, and it was by no means a one-off. Yet just 18 months before it would have taken me seven months of work to earn the same money.

I know some people get funny about it, and ask why I deserve it. But at the end of the day, you can't blame me for taking the opportunities that are offered to me – wouldn't you do the same? I'd be stupid if I didn't. And I work really hard for it – believe me, when there is an opportunity for me to make a success of myself, I am always working on it. But I'm not going to sit here and say I deserve it just because I work hard for it, because that would be disrespecting those who work just as hard in worthier jobs and who earn a lot less. But I have always been taught to take every chance that comes along, and whether it is fair on other people or not, this is about business. If I didn't take on jobs like this, someone else would. I am realistic about how long this might last. If it all ended tomorrow, at least I would know I had taken every opportunity that being in *TOWIE* has given me and set myself up for a good future.

9

THE BIGGER, THE BETTER

In Essex it really is a case of the bigger the hair, the better – which is a nightmare for me because my hair is really thin! But I have always found ways around that ... Although fashions do change when it comes to hair, right now it is all about volume, and it looks set to stay this way for a good while.

I love hair like the Kardashians have – yes, they are helped by extensions, but still, their hair looks so thick and healthy and shiny, with a great wave and volume. My hair is naturally dead straight, and like most people, I have always wanted what I can't have. I would love to have a wave in my hair, but no matter how much I try to make my hair curl at home, whatever product I use and however much effort I put in, I never get a really good curl.

I wanted a perm when I was younger, but I wasn't allowed. My mum had one though, and we always told her she looked like a poodle, so looking back, it was probably a good thing I didn't get one!

But even though I luckily avoided that mistake, I have not always known what to do with my hair. I don't think I have had any huge hair disasters, like done a Britney Spears and shaved my head or anything. But I can say it has not always looked the best.

When I was ten, I remember I did the spam ponytail or bun every day, religiously. If you have never had one, well, all I can say is well done on avoiding that mistake! But basically it was a ponytail or bun that was pulled back so much it gave you a spam forehead – when your forehead looks bigger than normal – because your skin was pulled back so tightly. Every hair was in place – and you made sure it stayed there by piling on loads of this minging gel. Yep, that look was an error.

You would have the ponytail or bun at the back, and then pull two bits of hair forward to hang down either side of your face. Those two bits of hair were very important – they pretty much made the look. It was inspired by Mel C, I guess, or at least she was a massive fan of it. As I've said before, although I always wanted to be Geri, I had a phase of copying Sporty Spice's look and walking around in a tracksuit all the time, and this hairstyle was a part of that.

Around the same time, Amy always put her hair in two low buns, just behind each ear, which we used to call two turds, because that's exactly what they looked like. I should probably stop there, shouldn't I? But before you judge her for that, just remember, we all learn from our mistakes!

But anyway, on to better hair days. I have perfected a

routine now for achieving big hair myself at home before I go out (see the box on pages 152–4). Or alternatively, if I have the time and the money, I do like treating myself to a blow-dry at the salon, and they will always make a good job of it.

I have experimented quite a lot with hair extensions to get volume in my hair. They are the one easy way to big hair – because you can literally double the amount of hair on your head. Extensions are a huge market now, and there are loads of different ways of attaching the hair, different types of hair – real or fake for a start – and a massive difference in prices, depending on what you are after.

One method that is really popular in Essex at the moment is Micro Rings Hair Extensions. Basically strips of hair are attached to your own hair with tiny metal rings that clamp onto your roots. There is no glue, or sewing, or braiding, like there is with other hair extensions, so it is supposed to be better for your own hair, and it is subtle. Once they are in, they are there to stay for quite a while as well, so you don't have to do anything more than get them tightened or replaced every few months.

They work for a lot of people, but I am not a fan of them really. I had them done just once, and it wasn't for me. Washing and blow-drying takes forever with them in. I like to wash my hair every day – it is so fine that it needs it, and I like my hair to be as clean and shiny as possible. But with the extensions in, it took about 90 minutes a day to do, and I really didn't want to spend that long on it, so it just annoyed me. Also I like to run my hands through my hair, which I couldn't do because of the little rings.

And no matter what is promised, extensions are always going

to be bad for your hair in one way or another. After I'd had the micro rings in for eight weeks, I could see that my hair was thinner and weaker. It's inevitable. So although it looks really good, do be aware that you are getting yourself into a cycle – the more you wear extensions, the more you need to keep wearing them. I'm not saying don't do it, as they can look great – just keep in mind that you might be doing damage in the long run.

After the micro rings, I used Hair Rehab London clip-ins. They are Lauren Pope's range and I love them. They are made from really thick, good-quality real hair, and are so simple to use. As the name implies, you just clip them onto your own hair in sections, wherever you want your hair to look thicker. Lauren has quite thin hair herself and has been trying out various extensions for years, and she has worked in modelling so she really knows what works and what doesn't.

She got her hair-range business up and running through a show called *Tycoon* a few years ago, where she was mentored by Peter Jones from *Dragons' Den*, which was great. Lauren is like me in that she has a good business mind and wants to do things outside of *TOWIE*. She is independent and wants to make money.

Like many beauty things though, extensions can get quite addictive. I used to put the clip-ins on just for special occasions or big nights out, then it got more and more often, then before I knew it I wouldn't even leave the house to have lunch with my friends without them. I only stopped using them as much when I went back to blonde this last time. At the moment, I am not using any extensions except for on really special occasions – I just do a lot of back-combing and use a lot of hairspray! I cut my hair into a bob earlier this year, as it had become so damaged from all the extensions, and I thought it was time to start again. And it worked! The hair that was left felt thicker and healthier, and it's easier to style.

I have also got more into wearing my hair up. The only problem is, I am not very good at doing it myself, so I tend to go to the salon. I like to have it quite tousled-looking, in a messy bun with a sweeping fringe. It's good to change your look sometimes – when celebrities rock the same hairstyles all the time, it can get a bit boring. I always think there is no excuse for a celeb to have bad hair, as looking good is half their job! Someone like Britney Spears, I can never understand. All that money, and yet her hair looks so dry and dead, and when she has extensions they look so badly done.

I also love my wigs – I have a right little collection going now, in different colours and styles. It's a good way of experimenting without having to do anything drastic to your own hair. I think they are really fun to wear, and can make an outfit. I'll leap on any excuse to get them out, like when we went to see *Priscilla Queen of the Desert* at the theatre. That was the perfect chance to get my pink bob going on!

Colour is a funny one for me. My natural colour is a kind of golden-brown, somewhere between brown and blonde, which is why my skin tone works with both shades, as do my eyebrows, which are also kind of in-between.

I didn't actually dye my hair much as a teenager – although as we were abroad so often, the sun would bleach it, so I looked like I had highlights long before I actually did.

In fact the first time I tried dyeing hair, it wasn't my own! My friend at school, Sarah, became my hair guinea pig, poor girl. I used to dye and cut her hair all the time, but we never did mine, so she ended up with all these awful hairstyles, while I got to try out what I wanted but still kept my own long hair!

It was only when I was 16 that Mum let me get highlights for the first time. She was quite strict about those kinds of things. I remember wanting to get my ears pierced ever since I was little, but she made me wait until I was ten years old for that, and she was the same about my hair – she had a set age in her mind that I had to be before I could start messing around with it too much.

I have also tried dyeing my hair red – I did that for my 18th birthday – but it didn't stay like that for long, as it was too hard to keep up. In fact I always seem to end up back at blonde.

I was blonde when I was doing modelling, and I was blonde when I started on *TOWIE* – I guess it is the colour I am most comfortable with. I am not a fan of bleach, or block colour, so I tend to have two or three different tones put through my hair at the same time, to give a more natural blonde look.

But when series three started, I decided I wanted a change. I guess I was thinking that I was single, it was a new series, and I wanted a new beginning. So I went dark. Not like goth-black or anything, just a nice chocolate-brown. I really liked it when I came out of the salon, and everyone kept telling me how much they loved it. It was really shiny, and looked exactly as I had hoped it would. I remember going on *Celebrity Juice* with Keith Lemon – which, by the way, was really good fun, although I was terrified! – and, looking back at that, I think my hair looked really good.

But then I decided to go a bit darker, and rather than going to the salon, I did it myself at home from a box. That wasn't so good, and it seemed to look even worse on TV. When the first episode of me with dark hair was aired, feedback on my looks became suddenly more, well, negative! Some people were still nice of course, but a lot of people were saying they preferred the blonde. And I could see where they were coming from. It was still bright and shiny in real life, but it looked really harsh against my skin tone on screen, and somehow the colour looked duller. I remember watching the beginning of the first episode, when Billie and I were in a bar together. Next to her bubbly blonde self, I just kind of disappeared. And that is not me! I am not a shy, hideaway girl.

So after seeing how it looked on screen for myself, I decided I really was a blonde at heart, and it was time to go back. I introduced the blonde gradually, over a couple of sessions in the salon, and I am more of a dark-gold blonde this time.

I don't think *Star* magazine were very pleased when I went back to blonde though – they had just got me and my dark hair into the studio the week before to do a whole new set of pictures to go at the top of my column. Oops, sorry about that!

I do think blondes have more fun

I think I will stay like this now – and before you ask, yes, I do think blondes have more fun!

I tend to get my roots done every five weeks. A girl called Polly comes to my house and does the highlights, and then puts toner on it to stop them being too bright. It's great, as she is happy to come round any time, so it fits with my lifestyle –

which doesn't exactly allow for routine. But while I am fussy about the colour, I am not too worried about the cut and am happy to let one of my friends cut it when I don't want to go to the salon. That's probably because I have never really had any hair nightmares. Like I've never been to the salon and come out with green hair or anything! I do remember once getting really upset because I asked for an inch off, and they took off three inches, but that is it. It grew back in a few weeks anyway.

I like having long hair, and it is my plan to grown it back – the bob is not here to stay! I had a bob with a fringe as a toddler too. After I started school, I just let it grow and grow, and by the time I left it was down to my waist. It was only when I was 18 that I cut it to the length it was until the start of this year. One of the reasons I like it long is that, as I mentioned earlier, I hate my ears. Honestly, they are really big! So I always try to cover the tips to make them look smaller. You are never going to see me with one of those little pixie haircuts or whatever. Can you imagine?

How to Get Perfect Big Hair Without Extensions

When I want my hair to look as natural as possible, this is how I get that big-hair effect.

- I put thickening or volume mousse in my hair, and brush it through with a big, round brush.

- Then I set my hair in rollers – I use five or six of them, and spread them out over my head. Heated rollers work best for me, but there are many different kinds – Jess Wright prefers the Velcro ones, for example. It's a question of trial and error to see what works best for you.

- After the rollers are in, I use a lot of hairspray – probably about half a can – and then leave it for an hour.

- After I take the rollers out, I run a wide-toothed comb through it. Some people get really curly hair at this point, but for me, because of the type of hair I have, the curls drop and it is more wavy.

- Then I part my hair at different points, sprinkle on some talc and rub it in. This helps give hair more volume, but make sure you only apply it at the roots.

- If I want really good volume, I backcomb my hair. Some people do this all over, but I think that is a bit much, so again I only do it at the roots, to give my hair more lift.

- Then I add a bit more hairspray, and I'm all done. If you have followed this routine exactly, I promise

➡

you it won't go limp within half an hour, but will really stay big and full of volume for the night.

- As with all these beauty treatments, if you have a big night out coming up and you can afford it, go to the salon! Most of the time, you won't be able to do it as well as the professionals.

Choosing the Right Hair Extensions

There is such a huge choice of hair extensions that choosing what to go for can be a pretty hard decision! But there are a few things you need to take into consideration.

The obvious one is whether you want them in for the long term, until you have them professionally removed or replaced, or if you just want them for a short while, to make a particular style look good for the night.

Then there is price. Fixed extensions cost more than clip-ins, and obviously the better quality the hair, the more it will cost. It's definitely worth forking out a bit, or you can end up with an irritated scalp, or hair that just doesn't look real.

If you are going for permanent extensions, really research the stylist – and where possible I would go for someone who specialises in extensions, rather than a hairdresser who just happens to do them on the side.

If you are buying clip-ins, spend a lot of time matching the colour to your own. A good shop will let you try them on, and a good internet shop will have a returns policy in case they don't quite match your own colour when you receive them. With clip-ins, people worry about what length to go for. I'd say always go longer than you think you'll need – you can always cut them once they are in place, just like normal hair. And if you are unsure, pay a hairdresser to put them in the first time and show you how to do it. It will be worth it!

How to Put in Clip-in Hair Extensions

Clip-in hair extensions are the only type you can put in yourself at home, and that's easy to do – once you know how. Here is my guide.

- Generally you will get six hairpieces – two medium pieces to go at the back of your head near the bottom, two large pieces to go further up your head at the back, and two small pieces to go at the sides.

- Start with your hair washed, combed and down, in the way you want it to sit.

- Part your hair across the bottom at the back using your fingers, just a bit above the bottom of your hairline, and clip in the first medium extension, attaching the clips as close to the scalp as possible. It doesn't matter if the parting is not perfectly straight – no one will see it.

- Repeat this with the other medium piece, a couple of inches above.

- The next parting should be just above the top of your ears, and the first of the larger extensions can be clipped in here, with the second a couple of inches above.

- The small sections are done in the same way at the side of your head. You can either do one on each side, or if you have a side parting and want one side to be thicker, you can add both to one side.

- Use a large brush with soft bristles to run through your hair afterwards to combine your hair with the extensions and create a natural overall look.

- When you take your extensions out, you need to treat them just as you would your own hair. So they need to be washed, conditioned, combed and dried in the same way.

- You can also curl and style them as you would your own hair – I find it easier to curl them before I put them on my head.

- Store them carefully! Brush them out and put them back in the packet, to keep them clean and dry.

- If you want to watch me explain this technique, there is a video on YouTube of me demonstrating on my own hair – put my name in the search bar and you will find it.

10

MY SISTER BILLIE

No book about me would be complete without a chapter on my sister Billie.

She has really influenced who I am as a person, and is my best friend as well as my sister.

She is only 11 months and 15 days older than me, so even in age we are really close. In fact we were born in the same year – she was born in January 1990, and I was born in December of that year. So we grew up pretty much side by side, and did everything together. We went to the same schools, went on family holidays together, swapped gossip and fashion, and shared the same friends. I don't think I have met another two sisters who are as close as me and Billie.

She is my best friend as well as my sister

We were also both really close to our mum growing up – in fact we are like three sisters, as Mum is so young. We hated to be apart from her when we were younger – Mum says that at one point she couldn't even go to the toilet without the pair of us appearing in the doorway, demanding to sit on her knee. She's a very tolerant lady!

We both got our confidence from our mum, I think, as she is a very strong woman. But Billie and I deal with the downsides of life quite differently. She likes to let it all out and talk and rant to people about things. I tend to keep things inside. I rarely cry in front of other people, not even my friends. If I am pissed off or upset, I will keep it to myself and then go off and cry on my own in my room. I keep my emotions hidden pretty deep inside so, for example, I'll talk openly with my friends about sex and that, but not the emotional side of my relationships. I think everyone saw that side of me when Mark or Joey and I had any conversations on the show that got too serious. I rarely put my feelings out there on show, and it was always me who would cut off the conversation when it got too deep. I am not sure why I do that, but it is me, and it is how I will always be, I think.

Billie always calls me Manf, rather than Samantha or Sam. My Auntie Sam is called Manf for short as well, so we are Big Manf and Little Manf! All our friends have copied Billie and call me that too, but the rest of my family still call me Min – short for Minnie.

When I got onto the show, Billie was 100 per cent happy for me. She thought it was great, and would help me choose my clothes and stuff like that. It really helped that I could talk to Billie about the things that were worrying me when *TOWIE* started, such as whether the real me was coming across.

Don't get me wrong, I loved spending loads of time with Amy on series one – like I said before, I think that was the best series for me – but I was seen very much as Amy's agony aunt, and I wanted the chance to show people what I was really like. So I thought it would be good to have some of my family on the show, so people could see other sides of me. I suggested Billie to the producers and brought her in to meet them, and they really liked her – she is as real as you can get. I really wanted to share the whole experience with her, and it has been great that we have been able to do that.

People always think I am the older sister, or that I am the one in charge, and possibly that's partly because I was on the show first and was more relaxed in front of the cameras, so I tended to take charge when they were around the two of us together at first. But the reality is that Billie definitely has the more overpowering personality out of the two of us!

She is fierier, and reacts on the spur of the moment, whereas I am softer and more laid-back, maybe too laid-back at times! I just let Billie get on with things. But we agree on most things anyway. For example, if we are deciding what to do with our day, we will always want to do the same things, and will come up with the same plan. The only time I might take the lead

> Billie is fierier and reacts on the spur of the moment, whereas I am softer and more laid-back

is if it's something to do with being brave. Say we are at a water park and there is a scary ride, Billie will wait for me to go on it first before she will go for it. I have to lead the way.

She was scared of a lot of things when we were little, like fireworks, and she would cry and climb into bed with me. One time Dad dressed up as Santa at Christmas to surprise us, but Billie was frightened of him and hid in my bed. I had to tell her it was Dad and not to worry!

I am about the only person she doesn't mind hugging, other than boyfriends. She is not a touchy-feely person – it annoys her – whereas as a kid, I would always want to be hugged.

We have both always been thoughtful about each other, about what would make the other happy. I remember when we were little kids and we'd be given £5 each to spend at the shops. We'd always make a deal that we'd spend it on each other, so we'd go off and come back with sweets and toys for each other.

We have the same humour, although Billie is definitely wittier than me – I'm not a funny person at all, annoyingly! She is also cleverer than me. While I was concentrating on sport at school, and my piano practice, she was good at her studies, especially English. We thought she might go to university, and she did stay on for sixth form, but then she decided to work instead. I think she saw me working and earning money, and realised she wanted to do the same.

Not that she is always sensible with her cash – that role falls to me! I have been saving all the money I've been earning from *TOWIE* and the life that has come with it to buy a house. It is something I have wanted to do for ages, and so I have worked towards that – and I finally got my dream home at the start of the year. It is a three-bedroom house with a garden and a big drive, just five minutes from Mum's house. It is the perfect place and I hope I am here a long time – maybe I'll even bring my kids up here!

I hadn't realised how much work it was to get the place in order though – I hired people to help and all my family chipped in. But it's been great having my own space, as well as my friends around all the time. Billie always comes over, and she loves the place, but it hasn't made her want to save for her own. She just spends what she has. Billie is much more someone who lives in the moment. So she is happy to live at Mum and Dad's for longer, if it means she can enjoy her life.

I am closer to Dad than Billie though. I am a real daddy's girl, whereas he and Billie argue a lot. Don't get me wrong, they love each other to bits, but they clash.

We did have a really happy childhood, despite any tough times we might have had – we just got on with it. I think too many people blame their upbringings for mistakes they make in their own lives, and become worse people because of it, but Billie and I don't. You would never have seen us rebelling at school, or being selfish, and then going 'Oh, it's cos it's hard at home' like some kids I knew did when their parents split up or whatever. No one is perfect, but we were always taught we made our own paths for ourselves.

But don't get me wrong, it is not all happy families between me and Billie – I can get pretty competitive with her!

I competed at swimming when I was younger – and when I was up against Billie, my competitiveness really came out! I remember that one year it was the last race of the season, and we were up against each other in the front-crawl race, and I won. To this day, she brings it up, and reckons I only won by a fingertip.

To be honest, I am probably too competitive at times. Whereas she was cool about who won in those situations, and would just be like 'Yeah, I've let the little sister win.' I'd go off to my room and sulk if I ever lost at anything to her – even silly things like board games!

Also, we can row. Like properly row. We have fewer rows now that we are older, but we used to really go at it like cat and dog. And I mean that literally – I used to bite her!

As I've said, I'm a really calm person and you won't get a reaction from me easily. But Billie will wind me up on purpose, just for a laugh. She will sit there and kind of mentally poke at me, until finally I'll snap. In the past that is when I would bite or punch her or throw a hairbrush at her. And you know what? Despite all the tormenting she did to get me to that point, once she got the reaction, she would be straight to Mum complaining, and I would look like the bad guy, because Mum wouldn't have seen the build-up.

Billie was smarter than me in rows, even when she was in the wrong. I remember her breaking my lava lamp once, and before I could get mad, she started crying, so then she got all the sympathy. Very clever, Billie!

Usually though, I know my limit, and when I should stop arguing. *Usually*. I remember one time when I was about 13 and she was annoying me. She kept on and on – I can't even remember what it was about – and I just kicked her to the floor and jumped on her back. Oh my God, she screamed, and I really thought I had broken her back! I was so scared that I had gone too far. It still didn't put a stop to our arguments though!

Neither of us like to apologise after a row. Billie might, if she realises she caused the argument by antagonising me, but I never say sorry. I refuse to! Normally what happens is we both just go off and sulk for half an hour and don't talk. Then we just go back to normal.

Our arguments when we were teenagers were never over anything important, just silly things we would get annoyed about. It was never over boys or anything – we never fancied the same guys luckily, and one of us was pretty much always in a relationship anyway. I can see why she fancies the guys she does, but they are never my type. Anyway it's one of those proper no-go areas, so you don't even think about it.

Our arguments when we were teenagers were never over anything important

There were times when Billie and I shared a bedroom. It wasn't cramped or anything – we had a double bed each, and our own bathroom – but it still meant that we were on top of each other and didn't have our own space. We also started sharing the same friends around this time, so we just weren't getting any time alone. Even when we were at friends' houses, we were together, so we were literally with each other 24 hours a day. Even the best of friends and closest of sisters are going to fight in that situation.

I remember one time Mark Wright came round, and Billie and I had a row and were screaming all sorts of abuse at each other. I think he was pretty shocked by it – shocked enough to tell his sister Jess about it anyway, and she still remembers him talking about it. I have stopped biting now though, I promise!

We have kind of grown out of the fighting now – at least the physical fighting anyway. The last time I can remember that happening I was about 15, and we had a proper scrap at my friend Ferne's house. I can't even remember what it was over. We were there for a sleepover, and I reckon Billie must have been showing off or something. We ended up punching each other, pulling each other's hair and really going for each other. It started off upstairs, and ended up downstairs. I think all our friends were shocked, and after that we realised that we had to grow out of this sort of thing.

Nowadays we only tend to argue about clothes and fashion. I believe in sharing clothes and shoes, whereas Billie is much more protective of her belongings. It drives me mad sometimes – why can't I borrow her things?!

I remember when I was 17 I was going to an Asian wedding, and I had no shoes to wear. She had these gold strappy ones that were perfect with my outfit, but she wouldn't let me borrow them, so I just took them. She went mad and it escalated into a huge row. I remember pushing her, running into the street and lobbing her shoes down the road. All over a pair of shoes. Like really?! I think – at least I hope – we are past that now!

We are quite different shapes anyway, so I guess it's not a bad thing that she doesn't like to lend her clothes to me. Billie's boobs are much bigger than mine. She's really conscious of them and tries to cover up her cleavage, which is mad – loads of people would love to have her boobs!

At least we've always really got on with each other's boy-friends over the years, which has been good. Billie has been with her current boyfriend, Greg, since September 2011. Before that she was with a guy called Dave for years, who was lovely, but the pair of them were so fiery, I couldn't keep up with whether they were madly in love or fighting! She's much calmer with Greg.

My last boyfriend, TJ, and Greg work together at a ticket agency and are best friends, so it was even better. The four of us would go out together all the time. We'd do everything together really, and it was a great set-up. I hope my next man gets on just as well with Billie's boyfriend!

11

DIET AND EXERCISE

Keeping my body in good shape is really important to me –
but doing regular exercise and eating healthily is not something I am good at, so this chapter is a bit of a hard one for me!
I always say I should be the last person to give advice on diet
and fitness, but then again, I am
generally quite happy with my
figure, and I get a lot of compliments about it, so I guess I must
be doing something right ...

Regular exercise and eating healthily is not something I am good at

As a kid, I was a little chubster. I
had a really fat face and stocky legs,
and even though I was well into sport at
primary school, it was only when I got to about 14 that my
weight suddenly fell away. I guess it was just puppy fat.

Now my weight varies a bit, but I try to keep a close eye on
it. The most it will vary, between my lightest and heaviest, is
a stone, and that is at my most extreme, and it doesn't go up

and down like a yo-yo or anything. I don't do anything to the extreme – like I don't spend every day in the gym, but nor do I veg in front of the TV all day, every day. It's the same with food – I'm not living off carrot sticks, but I'm not eating ten Mars bars a day either.

I am not self-conscious about my weight – I reckon so long as it is within reason, it is not something to overly worry about. It was weird seeing myself on screen for the first time though, because at certain angles you suddenly think you look fat, even though that might never have occurred to you before.

I am not self-conscious about my weight

It definitely had that effect on Lydia – after series one she became really serious about getting into shape, and hit the gym hard, using a personal trainer to help her drop from a size ten to an eight, and she became really toned. The change in her was amazing, and she has kept in shape ever since. Sadly I didn't feel the same motivation!

Anyway, as I've said, I was really into sport as a kid. The main one was probably gymnastics – I was actually training for the Olympic squad when I was at my best. That came about after Billie and I started going to a recreational gym class on Friday nights at Havering Gym Club.

It was just for fun in the beginning, but then they held trials for the club's training squad. Both Billie and I got through the trial, but as happens when you are kids, we didn't have time to do all the after-school activities we wanted, and had to pick and choose – and whereas I chose gymnastics, Billie chose

Brownies. So when she went off to her weekly meetings in her little brown dress, I was back-flipping my way around the gym. Although, I have to say, Billie definitely made the wrong choice. She hated Brownies, and thought the other girls bullied her. She had such a big row at a Brownie camp in Hastings once, over my mum's shepherd's pie – don't ask! – that Mum had to go and pick her up early. Not that gymnastics was easy – in fact it was pretty hardcore. We had sessions three days a week, for three hours at a time. An hour of that would be completely given over to strength work – sit-ups, press-ups, that kind of thing. I had a proper little six-pack back then! I think that's why I still have a pretty flat stomach today, because my muscles have retained some of their tone. Luckily for me!

Bearing in mind that I was probably only about nine at the time, the training was full-on. Girls would quite often end up in tears at the sessions, as although we really enjoyed it, there was a lot of pressure on us.

We were entered for competitions, and I was doing pretty well, but I had broken my arm twice and sprained it once, so it was weak and started to cause complications.

The first time I broke my arm, I was about five. I was standing on the kitchen counter, and my mum told me to get down. Of course, being strong-minded even then, I didn't! And, as if to prove that mums always know best, a minute later I fell off the counter backwards, got tangled between two chairs and my arm got caught and snapped. It was awful. I went to hospital and they put it in a cast for six weeks.

But if that wasn't bad enough, when I went back to have the

171

cast taken off, it turned out that it had been done wrong, and they had to break my arm again and reset it, so it was in a cast for another six weeks. How bad is that? So really, while you can blame me for the first break, the second was definitely not my fault … The upside, for me anyway, was that it was my right hand, and I am right-handed, so I got six weeks off school, as there was no point me going in when I couldn't write. Then, when I was doing gymnastics, I sprained the same arm on the trampoline, and put it out of action for a few more weeks. So, all in all, my right arm was not destined for gymnastics, even if the rest of me thought I was!

I remember that at one point I trained with two Bulgarians called Buba and Svet, who were lovely, and I was actually supposed to go to Bulgaria for five weeks for training. I think that is when it would have moved up a gear – if I had done that, I'd have been into even more serious training, and to be honest, I wasn't up for it. I was getting into life at secondary school by then, and was starting to want to go out. I wanted to spend my weekends seeing friends, not putting time into even more training. Also, with my weak arm, I knew I was never going to be at the top. Mum was happy for me to stop too – she never pushed me into doing it, although she was really happy and overwhelmed when I was doing well. She knew that if I wasn't enjoying it so much anymore, my time was up.

I was so glad I did it for that time though. It was a great experience, and I met some of the world's best gymnasts. I still kept it up at school afterwards, along with plenty of other sports. I did PE as one of my GCSEs, and was also in the netball and swimming teams, and I loved rounders. I don't understand why, but no one takes rounders very seriously in this country, which is a shame as it is probably my favourite sport.

I also did diving classes outside of school, and swam at a club called the Killer Whales in Hornchurch. Netball was pretty funny at primary school – because my mum was the coach! Raphael Junior School was so tiny that practically the whole class was in the team in each year! Mum came in and coached us on a voluntary basis. I have to say, I was one of the best players, and was always Goal Attack or Wing Attack because I was fast and whippy.

I quite miss playing netball actually. My friends and I are always talking about setting up a team now, to play just for fun. It's great in the winter. I'd never want to go out in the cold for a run, but netball is different. Netball really works all your muscles, with all the turning and stretching, and I reckon it's one of the best sports for keeping fit. I played a match a year or two back for a team of models, and I ached for days afterwards, as I was out of practice. I'd also forgotten how vicious it can get! Don't let any boy claim it is not a tough sport – they have clearly never seen a game when really competitive girls are on the court!

But all the exercise I was doing was very tied in with school. Once I left at 16, I suddenly found I wasn't doing any sport at all, so instead I began to walk a lot. I would catch the train to work from Brentwood every day, and it is about a mile and a half's walk from my house to the station – uphill on the way back! It meant that I was doing 50 minutes of exercise every day, and actually I found that was enough to keep me in shape, so for a while I was getting away with it.

But since I left my job and started on *TOWIE* it has been harder. I'm afraid I do no regular exercise at all! Even walking is out as, I'll be honest, I drive or get cabs everywhere.

I have joined the gym twice, but it just isn't for me, and I'd rather go swimming or for a bike ride if I had to. What happens when I go to the gym is that I'll really go at it for a few weeks and lose four or five pounds, but then I get bored and give it up. I just can't keep up the momentum. The only time I am happy to go is before a holiday because then I am only aiming to do it for a short burst, so I can focus and get to a size eight within a short time.

I have noticed a difference without the constant exercise in my life though. Whereas I was pretty much always a size eight before I started on *TOWIE*, now I swing between an eight and a ten. And although my perfect weight is probably just over 9st, at times I creep up to 9st 7lbs before I realise and do something to pull it back down. Don't get me wrong, that is not overweight for my height – I am five foot six, so I am supposed to weigh between 9st and 10st 4lbs – but for me my ideal weight is around 9st.

I just feel like I never have time to fit exercise in now. Whenever I get a few hours off, I am knackered. It's especially hard in winter, when I just want to be warm indoors. Going out and getting fit is the last thing on my mind when it's cold outside.

I also think that some of my weight gain is probably just part of getting older. My body is more adult now, and I like my curves, so I don't really mind. I look more like a woman than a teenager now.

Obviously everyone has their own preference, and the main thing is feeling comfortable and happy with your body, whatever shape you are, but personally I would never want to be skinny. I think very skinny legs, where you can see a big gap between a girl's thighs, are not nice at all. Having hips and legs with a bit of shape is definitely the best look when you are in a bikini.

> *The main thing is feeling comfortable and happy with your body*

As for boobs, again everyone has their own preference, but I quite like mine, because they add a bit of curve, and it means I am in proportion with the rest of my body. I am a 32D, which I think is about right for my age and size.

As I've said, the one place I can never lose weight from is my arms. They stay chunky even when I lose weight, and no matter what I do, they are kind of bulky. But I guess I have just learned to put up with them. My legs are also never going to be skinny, but I don't mind that. I have always had pretty stocky thighs, even when I was little, so that's not going to change.

If I put on weight on my belly or face or anywhere else, I can lose it pretty easily, but that's not the case with my thighs and arms. But that's fine – I'm never going to be skinny, but I don't want to be, and I've never had any complaints about my curves!

I actually think girls are a lot more likely to judge each other's figures than guys are. That is probably one of the reasons you won't catch me doing those magazine articles where you talk about your body hang-ups, or pose naked to have your body analysed. I did do something like that once for a magazine, and posed in a bikini, and I was described as athletic and curvy, which I was fine with. I had been going to the gym for a while before that shoot, and was more confident about myself, but I still can't say I felt comfortable with it.

The most exercise I do now is when I go clubbing and dance all night – that has to count as good exercise, right? The only downside is that I will have a few drinks when I go clubbing, and obviously alcohol is not great when you're watching your weight. I have definitely noticed that I've put on weight since I began drinking and socialising more. It's a case of moderation, I guess. I'm quite a fan of Amaretto and Diet Coke, and vodka, lime and soda is another favourite. I like to drink white wine with ice cubes in it with food.

I don't have strict dos and don'ts as far as food and diet goes. The only thing I do try to stick to – and I know loads of people say the same – is to drink plenty of water. It makes such a difference to your skin. I look at my mum, who drinks two pints of it religiously every day, and she looks so young. She doesn't look her age at all – she is 42, but people always think she is our older sister.

My one big downfall is Chinese takeaways. When I lived at home with my mum, dad and Billie, I'd say we'd order one in once a week. Noodles, rice, chicken strips, prawns ... even chips. We'd go for the full works! I still make a point of going back for a Chinese even now, or getting them round to mine for one on a Friday night.

Generally, though, my mum makes pretty healthy food. She

is really conscious to make things from scratch and to avoid ready-made meals. I want to do the same now that I've moved out of home – my only problem, as you might have noticed on *TOWIE*, is I can't cook! The one time we tried to cook food for a Christmas party at Arg's, Amy, Harry and I didn't exactly pull it off very well. And then when Mark took me on a date to learn to cook, and the chef

I don't have strict dos and don'ts as far as food and diet goes – my one big downfall is Chinese takeaways

slapped this bloody great dead fish onto the counter ... well, that was it! There was no chance I was going to cut off its head or gut it. I like good food, and I don't mind giving things a go, but really, there is a limit! I guess I'll be forced to learn when I live on my own though, for the sake of my health and weight.

My typical daily diet starts with a cup of tea in bed, and a biscuit – either a chocolate digestive or one of those Viennese ones from Marks & Spencer. I love them! I know it is not the best way to start the day, but I have to have it. Mum used to bring it up for me, and missing out on that is one of the real downsides of leaving home! In fact bringing me my daily tea and biscuit in the morning is probably my main require-ment in any boyfriend who wants to stand a chance of lasting long ...

Then, after I have got up and had my shower and that, I will have breakfast. Normally it is whatever cereal is in the cupboard, like Frosties, Sugar Puffs, or Coco Pops, with semi-skimmed milk. Or if I want something different, I have a slice of toast with peanut butter or Marmite. Hovis Best of Both bread, if you really want to know!

Then for lunch I have a sandwich and a packet of crisps, or sushi and a packet of crisps. The crisps are non-negotiable. But I make up for it with some kind of fruit afterwards. And I generally just drink water with lunch.

When I lived at home, dinner was basically whatever Mum made, so a roast, or pasta, or fish and veg. Since I moved out I have tried to cook a few meals – I've done steak, and lamb chops with veg. TJ cooked a bit in the beginning, and Mum still comes round with food.

Snack-wise, I had loads of intentions to just fill my house with healthy food, but I'll be honest, I'm already failing! I have the odd bit of fruit or a yoghurt, but there are a lot of crisps. And takeaways still feature pretty regularly in my diet . . . I didn't realise how expensive food was until I started buying it for myself though – I'm going to have to curb my addiction to shopping in Marks & Spencer!

After series two of *TOWIE* my weight crept up to 9st 7lbs, which is the heaviest I have ever been. I had just been to Marbella, and I think the partying and lack of exercise was beginning to show. I tend to have a pretty good sense of when I have put on weight, even without checking it on the scales, as my clothes will feel tighter and I'll just generally feel bloated and heavy. And that's what happened after Marbella – I felt bigger, and suddenly my size eight clothes were too tight.

So I tried to be healthy to get ready for the third series. I did that by just making small changes, like not having butter on my toast, having a salad instead of a sandwich for lunch, taking smaller portions at dinner, and swapping my morning cereal for eggs. I don't know that much about dieting though, so when I am trying to lose weight, I will print something off the internet and try to follow that. I've always wanted to try the Cambridge Diet – where you replace food with milkshakes, as I like milkshakes, so think I would find that one easy! But you have to be a certain amount overweight to do it, and sadly – or rather happily – I'm not.

I tried going to a boot camp once. I went for just one day and, I have to say, I hated it. Being bossed around like I was in the army was not my kind of thing – I hate being told what to do. It is scary being shouted at like that, and there is just no leeway. You do what they say, and that's it. And they always make you do more than you feel you can – like they'll tell you to do ten repetitions of something, then when you are completely exhausted and think you are coming to the end of it, they suddenly go 'Right, three more.' I don't think that's fair!

The one I did was the Trimmer You Boot Camp, and I went to their centre in the Peak District with *Love It* magazine to do a feature. The daily routine started when you had to get up at 6 a.m. for an hour's run. Grim. Then you were given some water and nuts before you did another workout. And only after that could you have breakfast – if you can call it breakfast! I was so unimpressed by it – it was like a spoonful of porridge or something, along with a quarter of a banana and some herbal tea. I am a big eater, and that did not impress me!

Lunch and dinner were nicer, but the portions were so tiny, it really put me off. I know you are supposed to be losing weight, but you need food to give you the energy to get through all the exercise. I might have liked it more if they hadn't totally starved us. Then there was an evening walk, which was a nice way to unwind at the end of the day, although by then all you wanted to do was sleep!

Most of the cast have been to boot camps at some point, but from what I have heard theirs were all pretty basic, whereas mine was an exclusive – and expensive – one. The facilities were lovely, and you could unwind at night with a Jacuzzi in your room. I guess that was the best bit.

I wouldn't totally knock them – they are a good option if you are the kind of person who needs to be bossed into doing something, or you want to lose a few pounds and shape up quickly – but it just isn't for me.

I'm not sure it was great for Arg and Gemma either. They both lost weight at boot camps – then put it back on again. They need longer-term targets over a few months. Arg especially is a yo-yo dieter. He does try, but basically, he is a bit greedy! He thinks it is rude to leave food, so he always finishes his, and then if you have left any, he starts to pick at that as well. It's a bad habit.

The one bit of intense blitzing since starting *TOWIE*, when I really noticed a big difference and enjoyed myself in the process, was when Billie, Lydia and I made a fitness DVD called *The Essexercise Workout*.

There are three 20-minute sections in it: Totally Retro Reem, which is a dance workout; No Carbs Before Marbs, which is combat training; and the Well Jel Workout, which is cardio. We were working on the video for five days solid, and it was exhausting, but great fun. We spent the first three days learning the routines with the lady who was organising it – who, I swear, must have had close to 0 per cent body fat. She wasn't horribly skinny or anything, because she was toned and muscly, but you could not have pinched even a tiny bit of fat on her body. Then there was our instructor, Glenn Ball who, I have to say, is pretty fit, in both meanings of the word ... He certainly gave us something to look forward to each day anyway!

No carbs before Marbs!

After he had taught us the routines and we had got them perfected, we spent two days filming it. We were doing exercise non-stop, from 9 a.m. to 5 p.m. every day, and it was exhausting, great fun and very hardcore.

I remember wanting a sausage sandwich on the first day of filming, and the others asked for bacon sandwiches. But you'd think we had asked for someone to be shot or something. Honestly! The room went silent, and we were pointed towards this amazing but healthy food they had got for us, like fruit and nuts and that. But we had been out the night before and had not had dinner, so I really wanted proper food, and stood my ground.

Eventually they had to go and check with the boss if it was allowed, and there was a ten-minute debate, and then I was told that for health and safety reasons it wasn't a great idea. I know that exercising straight after food isn't ideal, but I was desperate and was determined to get my sausage sandwich!

Eventually they gave in and it was allowed, but wow, the way we worked out, I think I burned it off again in five minutes anyway.

By the end of the five days my old six-pack was starting to reappear, and the definition in my muscles was showing again. I think that is an upside of all the sport I did as a kid – as soon as I start to exercise again, my muscle tone improves very quickly. I think an athletic figure is very attractive. Don't get me wrong, I don't want to go all body builder-esque, like Jodie Marsh, but looking like you are toned and in shape is great.

Sadly, once filming for the DVD ended, I didn't keep it up – until the DVD came out that is, and then I used it to get back in shape again! That was the weirdest thing, following myself on the screen, but it was a really funny way to do it.

I think Lucy Meck has the best body on the show. She is naturally slim, and while she isn't really into exercise, she eats well.

One person on the show who I can see worries about her body all the time, and who really shouldn't, is Jess. She is so beautiful and slim – slimmer than me – but she is so insecure. Insecurities are natural, but she has a lot, and I don't think she is fair on herself. I don't know where it comes from really, as she has a supportive family, a successful business and a great body! But the smallest things stress her out. It's silly because people are always complimenting her looks, and she's got a perfect shape, even though she doesn't go to the gym and really likes her food and wine! It's her insecurities that made her get her boobs done, although I thought they were good before. Now she worries they are too big. You can't win!

Out of other celebs, I'd probably say Eva Mendes has my dream figure. She is slim, but still curvy, and that, for me, is always a good look. I also think – like probably every girl in the country – that Abbey Clancy has an amazing figure, even after having a baby. But while it works for her, I think her frame would be too skinny on most people, and is not necessarily a body shape to aspire to.

When it comes to my family, Mum is a naturally tall and slim person. Looking back at her old photos, she has always been skinny. My biological dad is more of a muscular figure. I reckon I am somewhere in between. Billie is smaller and curvier than me. She has bigger hips and boobs, and where I am an eight to ten, she is a ten. Though that's mainly because of her boobs! She takes after Nanny Wendy – our biological dad's mum. I don't think either of us envy each other's figures. We just see them for what they are – both the advantages and disadvantages, and we have always been brought up to be proud of them.

12

THE OTHER WAY
IS MARBS

No book about me – or any of the *TOWIE* lot for that matter – would be complete without a chapter on Marbella. It is like a home away from home for me and loads of Essex people, and I reckon I could go there every year for the rest of my life and never get bored of it.

If you don't know it, Marbella – or Marbs, as we call it – is a city in the south of Spain, but while the weather might be much nicer than at home, the mentality there really is the same as in Essex, and the lifestyle suits us perfectly. It's as if someone's transported everyone from Essex onto the beach!

You can see from *TOWIE* how much of a part Marbs plays in our lives. When it starts to get closer to party season, and people are sorting out their trips, there is an immense amount of planning going on, as everyone makes a real effort in the run-up to their holidays.

As Marbs is all about posing, everyone wants to get in

shape. That's why that famous *TOWIE* saying came about – 'No Carbs Before Marbs!' Ellie Redman came up with it on the show as a motivational saying when she was running a diet class for Arg, and it just kind of stuck.

Back in the day, Marbella was a more exclusive, expensive resort. Everyone there had money, and it was more likely to be filled with Arab sheiks and billionaire businessmen than Essex girls and boys on holiday. But in recent years it has become more known for its partying, although still in a classy way. It is like a posh Magaluf! So rather than going out on a night in shorts and flip-flops, you will find that people make a real effort, in glamorous dresses and heels. And it is still very expensive. You have to have money to go there. I would say that for a five-day holiday, even for girls – who generally get a lot for free or paid for them out there – you should allow at least £1,000. Drinks are really expensive too, so there is still an exclusive feel to the bars and clubs.

Marbella has become known for its partying

We used to go on holiday there when Billie and I were little. I have loads of lovely memories of us going as a family and just relaxing on the beach, going for nice meals and playing around the pool. When we were kids, there was a place called the Ocean Club, which was a gorgeous private pool and sunbathing area. Now it is home to a big party each bank holiday, with huge white beds and everyone spraying champagne at each other at 5 p.m. It is one of the most exclusive places to go, and if you want to get noticed in Marbella, that is where you have to be. The way the Ocean Club has changed shows exactly how Marbella has changed from upmarket and family-orientated, to still upmarket, but more party-focused.

I'm not sure what actually caused the change in Marbella, but at some point the clubs that held nights in Essex, such as Love Juice, Sintillate and Unique Parties (which was the name of Mark Wright's party nights), started holding nights in Marbs too, and it was like the Essex crowd just followed them out there. So before you knew it, half the county was over there, for the bank holidays originally, and then it extended into the whole summer season.

I always go out with my girl mates, and end up in the same hotel as loads of people I know, Hotel PYR, in the centre of Puerto Banus. Mark and his mates are normally there too, and we try to get rooms near each other. It can descend into carnage. It's like half the people I went to school with are out there. In fact a lot of people I don't have time to catch up with back in Brentwood, I catch up with in Marbs!

The boys go a bit mental when they are there, and do some proper disgusting things. I remember them pooing in each other's bags, and one of them putting Josh's (Mark's brother) toothbrush up their bum. He realised what had happened before he used it, but still! Once Lydia and Arg fell out, and Mark told Arg to play hard to get, but it backfired and she just didn't talk to him, so Arg stayed in the hotel for two nights, sulking. We found Mark weeing on Arg's bed after the second night, saying it was revenge for him staying in. It was all really childish.

Mark really thinks he is Mr Marbella. He is so worried about his image over there, and loves to think he is the centre

Mark really thinks he is Mr Marbella!

of it all. I remember one night the girls and I were standing on the balcony blowing a foghorn we had found, and he went mad, yelling at us that it was Marbella, not Magaluf!

It's a funny place really, Marbs. So much of it is about image and posing. People will be strutting around the pool in diamante bikinis and heels, wanting to know where each person had bought their outfit. And no way could you be seen in the same bikini two days in a row. That would be the ultimate mistake! The big hair is also out in force, and everyone gets properly made-up.

But actually all that effort is just to look good at the start of the evening for the photographs – by the end of the night, it is all forgotten, as it is impossible to keep looking glam and on top form at a pool party. So after a few drinks, people's true colours and sense of fun come out. By the time everyone is going home, they have flat hair and their lashes have been left behind, floating in the pool. Classy! But memorable – if you haven't drunk too much.

There is always a lot of scandal and rumour going around Marbella. The same as back home in Essex, everyone loves a good gossip when they are out in Spain. So if you talk to a boy in, say, Sinatras or some other club one night, by the next day, everyone is saying you went back to your apartment with the guy. Everything gets exaggerated. Then again, there is a lot of that kind of thing going on – the *TOWIE* boys definitely don't go home without a girl when they are out there because so many people are up for it. There is a real holiday vibe of everyone just being up for a good time and letting their guards down a bit more than they do in the UK.

Take Arg, for example, who I have known for years. I love him to pieces, and hope we will always be friends. But he was always the single one out of his group of friends, and the rest always had girlfriends. He was the cuddly, nice one, who everyone loved being around, but no one wanted to date.

I always used to feel sorry for him and would dance with him when I saw him at Faces nightclub or wherever. We'd be like grinding together, but my boyfriend at the time didn't mind, because he knew it was just Arg and we were all friends. Arg and I laugh about it now.

But then Lydia came along, and suddenly she was his girlfriend – it was a proper whirlwind. Everyone was like 'Oh my God, no way, she is too good for him! I can't believe he has done it!' Arg didn't mind though – he is good at taking jokes like that. Lydia was the first person Arg slept with, although I'm not sure if Arg was her first.

But then they went to Marbella, and he cheated on her. I'm not sure exactly what happened – he told her it was just a kiss, although Marbs rumours are that he had sex with the other girl. But, as I said, everything gets exaggerated out there, so who knows what to believe! Although it was discussed in series one, we never found out the truth. And I'm not sure Lydia has exactly been a saint either. My point is just that even those two, who are really tight, were tempted to stray when they were out there, as it is that kind of place.

As for Mark, he is shameless when he is out there. I know that it's not as if she has much of a choice, but Lauren has been very naïve over the years, letting him go to Marbs on his own. Take those pictures that came out in the summer of 2011, of him naked on the apartment balcony while Lucy Meck was in the room. Did she really think nothing had happened? Talk about kidding herself!

The first time I was allowed to go to Marbs with my friends rather than my parents was when I was 17. The year before, Billie had been allowed to go away with her friends, and they went to Magaluf, but I wasn't allowed. I was so mad! But once I hit 17, off to Marbs we went. Other than a few holidays elsewhere with boyfriends, it's always been about Marbella since then. I go at least three times a year, for two weeks at a time if I can – a week of partying, then a week of relaxing. My grandparents live about half an hour away from Marbella, so I go and see them as well. I've got quite a good set-up going!

It's weird because each year you see the next wave of younger people coming out. It's like a rite of passage you have to go through when you hit 16 if you want to be proper Essex! A lot of people say the recent publicity for the place is making it go downhill, but either way, I can say I have had some of the best times of my life there, and I have some great memories.

Last year I went to Ibiza for the first time, and I'm not going to lie – I loved it. It was a class above Marbella in a way, and I can see it having a bit of a comeback. We had an apartment overlooking Bora Bora beach, and I loved waking up in the morning and seeing people still partying from the night before. It's great because people still make an effort, but not too much. Looking good is not the only thing they are there for. Sometimes that side of things can get a bit much in Marbs, so Ibiza made a nice change.

My next plan is to go to Vegas with some girls I went to school with. We have wanted to go for ages, but I am the youngest, so they have had to wait for me to turn 21 before we could plan the trip, because you can't drink until you are 21 in the States. We have had a few meetings to plan it already, because we want to get it right. We want a big penthouse apartment in the middle of Vegas. How amazing will that be? I can't wait until I'm in a casino out there, with a cocktail in my hand …

I went to LA a while ago, for the TV quiz show *Scream If You Know the Answer*, and I loved it. No one knew who I was, but I was still treated like a celeb – the customer service there is amazing. I can see why a lot of people end up moving over there. Who knows? Maybe I will one day!

The other place that is becoming more popular among the Essex crowd is Dubai. Marbella is for the posing and partying, and Dubai is for couples or those who want a more chilled-out holiday. It's obviously further away, but it is hot all year round, and is shamelessly glamorous and luxurious, which is just what we like!

I went there in 2011 for the first time, and loved it. I went with Jess Wright, and we stayed in the Grosvenor House hotel in the Marina area. We were there for the opening of our friend Mark Fuller's Embassy club, and the whole night just summed up the city. The club has a gorgeous view over Dubai – it is on the 45th floor, higher than any club in the UK. And everything was that little bit more extravagant too – the food and drink, the glamour of the place, the effort people put into their outfits ... it suited me perfectly! Billie has been out there a few times, and she loves it too. I hope to go back there regularly now.

So these are the places that seem to have a closer link to Essex than most. It is almost like you can see little pockets of Essex around the planet.

Essex is a totally unique, amazing place, and I wouldn't be happy with anyone who disagrees with me about that! The people, the mentality, the fashion ... Everything about Essex really gives the place its own identity that people all around the UK instantly recognise.

The county really is like a little bubble within the UK. I know it sounds stupid, but when I leave Essex, I honestly expect everywhere else to be totally different, like I have gone to a different country or something. And actually, most of the time it is! When I do personal appearances and that around the country, I am always surprised by other areas. I can't always explain it, but when I was in Glasgow, for example, I felt like I was on another planet, because it was so different from Essex!

Actually, when I say Essex, what I mean is only a small part of it. That's what all the *TOWIE* people mean when we talk about Essex. For us, the true Essex is only a small part of the county – Brentwood, Loughton, Buckhurst and Chigwell, and the smaller places nearby. They are the centre of the real Essex mentality – and, to be honest, I don't think the other parts have quite the same thing going for them.

Anyway, I'm not sure what has made Essex like it is, but I know people have a real loyalty to the area. A lot of families have lived here for generations, and wouldn't think of moving anywhere else. So because of that, a lot of people know each other and have relatives living nearby. It's great and definitely makes for a closeness and sense of community, but the downside of that is sometimes it can feel a bit too incestuous. Like if you date someone, chances are they have dated one of your friends, or they are friends with your ex, or your cousin, and so on. It also means it is pretty hard to keep any secrets! You can see that with my own love life. The minute Mark and I even started to talk about going on a date in series three, for example, it was only a matter of hours before people were reporting it back to Joey and stirring things up.

On *TOWIE* some scenes are set up to get a reaction for entertainment reasons – like someone will be encouraged by the producers to go on a night out to a certain bar without knowing why, then they will find their ex is there with a new partner. Then of course it kicks off! So their reaction is real, but the actual scenario has been set up. The fact is though, because of the incestuous nature of the Essex community, that is not much different from how it really is. The chances are that if I went for a drink with a guy, someone he or I know would be there, and would tell other people they had seen us. Before you know it, everyone knows your business and has an opinion on whether you should get married or not!

Family is really important in Essex – we are probably quite old-fashioned in that way, but families tend to be very close-knit. Everyone sticks together, and there doesn't seem to be so much of a generation gap between parents and their kids that I see outside of Essex. For example, even as a teenager, I'd have thought nothing of going for dinner and drinks with my parents – it can be a good night out! But teenagers elsewhere seem to have the mentality that they wouldn't be seen dead doing that. In Essex people are generally proud of their families.

Look at the Wright family, for example. I love them. They all have such total love and respect for Nanny Pat, and she clearly does for them. She is great and has the best sense of humour and so many stories to tell – she really has 'been there, done that', and she is a proper credit to the family. And Carol would do anything for her kids – Mark and Jess, who are on the show, and also Natalya and Josh, who aren't – and is so proud of them. Proud mums are brilliant – mine is the same! It is obvious the Wrights all love each other loads. For me, they really represent a true Essex family.

Another true Essex sentiment is a real loyalty to the area. While people from Essex can criticise it, people from outside are not allowed to! There is nothing more annoying than people who have never been, going on about Essex stereotypes. It is definitely no one else's place to pass judgement – especially when they are wrong! So yeah, Essex people are fiercely proud of their roots, and will always defend their county.

When it comes to the ultimate Essex girl's icon – that's a tough one. It is easier to come up with the ultimate Essex guy's hero, who I reckon would be Lord Sugar. He is this guy who started with nothing, and now look where he is – pretty inspirational! Although I have to say, he did annoy me when he slagged off *TOWIE*, calling it 'atrocious'. I would have thought he would remember his own roots, and what it is like when you are starting out and trying to get a foot in the door.

I was like 'Wait a minute, where did you start out?' I think that, business-wise, a lot of the cast are probably doing better than he was at our age anyway. I reckon I have earned more money in the last year than he did when he was my age. So I thought it was a shame that he had to go and slag us off when we were just aiming to be like him.

As far as girls go, if I had to pick an icon, it would probably be Victoria Beckham. She is not quite the perfect idol, but she did start here from nothing, and now look what she has achieved. And let's face it, most of us would be happy to be living her life, especially if you got David thrown in!

One person who is definitely not an inspirational Essex girl is Jodie Marsh. Oh my God, she got us all such a bad name on that *Essex Wives* show. That was a bad year for Essex! But she doesn't represent the county at all. There are girls like her all over the UK – sadly!

Thinking about other areas of the UK, the place most similar to Essex I'd say is Liverpool. But it is like an exaggerated Essex, so the tans are deeper, the hair is bigger and the make-up is heavier. Even the partying is more extreme. So whereas we will go out at 8 or 9 p.m. and get home at 2 a.m., after going to one bar and one club, they go out at midnight, go to bar, after bar, after bar, and then several clubs, before getting home at 6 a.m. It is hardcore, and I don't know how they do it! It is like being permanently on holiday.

I feel quite relaxed with Scousers. Personality-wise, and in the loyalty they feel for where they are from, they are like us. The main difference I see is that they are more hyperactive. Sometimes it is too much, and I get a bit overwhelmed when

I am there. Essex people are more laid-back. Scousers seem to put all their energy into partying and having fun, whereas an Essex girl wants to do well in life, so will be concentrating on work and how to improve herself.

My favourite Liverpudlian girl is Gemma Merna. She is stunning, and knows how to have fun without going totally mental. We were introduced by my manager, Adam, as he looks after her as well, and we just clicked. We don't see each other that often, but we text and tweet a lot, and if we are in the same town we will go out for dinner and drinks.

The Scousers know how to put effort into their appearance too. They have a similar fashion sense to us, although obviously not as good! They seem to like similar things to us, but don't pull them off quite as well, or with as much class. Their fashion is also not as up to date, so as we are growing out of something, they are starting to like it.

And, oh my God, one thing I don't get about Scousers is this thing of wearing your hair in rollers out on the town during the day. Apparently it is just so that their hair can set in time for a night out, but it has become like this weird fashion that no one outside Liverpool seems to understand. And actually, I don't think the lads up there get it either, from what they have said to me!

I have been photographed with my hair in rollers a few times, but that has just been on the way to filming. It has been me not having enough time to get ready at home and being practical – it definitely wasn't a fashion statement! Apparently Coleen Rooney and Alex Curran were spotted doing it first, and now everyone is at it in the shopping centres. There are a lot of WAG wannabes in Liverpool. I guess they are a lot more like celebrities up there than they are down in Essex. Down here, if you go out with a footballer, you tend to keep it a bit on the down-low. I guess it's because we are so close to London, and you see so many A-list stars there that it is not a big deal to see a footballer, whereas in Liverpool the foot-ballers and WAGs are the biggest celebs.

You see it on that show on E4, *Desperate Scousewives*. No one out-side Liverpool had heard of one of the main girls, Amanda Harrington, and yet it seems she is famous in Liverpool. I'm asked about that show a lot, and while I don't want to slag it off – it had some good bits to it – at the end of the day, we did it first, and they were just copying us. The original will always be the best. The fact that locals were not fans of it doesn't reflect well either, and I'm not really surprised the series hasn't been recommissioned. With us, it's different, and you will find most people in Essex are fans and appreciate the way we are representing the area.

The Top Ten Places to Visit in Marbella

If you are heading over to the Essex home away from home, these are my favourite places that you should be sure to visit:

I. Nikki Beach, Playa Don Carlos, Elviria. This beach club is world-famous for a reason. It is huge and exclusive, serves amazing food and hosts fantastic parties. Great for celeb-spotting too!

2. The Ocean Club, Avenida de Lola Flores, Puerto Banus. Based around a pool, this is a more laid-back and sophisticated place to go. It is also where the infamous spray parties happen. See you there on the next bank holiday!

3. Buddha Beach, Villa Marbella Urb, Puerto Banus. This is like everything you could possibly want rolled into one: a gorgeous pool, beach, restaurant and spa all in the same place. You could spend every day of your holiday here and be happy.

4. Funky Buddha, Camino de la Cruz, Marbella. This glam club is a great place to party into the night. Wear your best outfit when you head here.

5. TIBU Banus, Antonio Banderas Square, Puerto Banus. A sophisticated club full of beautiful people. Book a table and make the most of the waitress service.

6. Pangea, Calle Muelle Benabola, Puerto Banus. A drink on the roof-top terrace here is a must, just to see the amazing views over the marina and out to sea.

7. Olivia Valere, Istan Road, Marbella. This restaurant and club feels really exclusive in an old-fashioned Hollywood kind of way. Love it!

8. Ristorante Regina, Nueva Andalucia. I love this place when I want a more relaxed night out. There is live music playing while you eat the fab Italian food. It is about five minutes out of town – but well worth the effort!

9. Sisu Boutique Hotel, Nueva Andalucia, Puerto Banus. This hotel is definitely the place to be seen and has great pool parties during the day. Be warned, you won't get much sleep though, so only stay there if you are up for non-stop partying! Coming down to breakfast to find people already drinking is not unusual.

10. Plaza Beach, Puerto Banus. I go here pretty much every day when I'm in Marbs. You get some great food while chilling on the beach and listening to the tunes that are pumping out every day. Lively and central to the action, there is also a Park Plaza Hotel overlooking the beach that is great, although be prepared to pose if you stay there!

13

CHANGING *TOWIE* AND THE FUTURE

There is no question about how well *TOWIE* has done – we never dreamed when we started out that we would end up with an award-winning show that gets 1.8 million viewers, and looks set to stretch to many more series.

Not just that, but it has become an actual brand in its own right – walking round the shops, I see *TOWIE* stuff everywhere: our Christmas cards in the newsagent, our DVDs in the video shop, our bronzer on the make-up counters ... And that's when I can actually get around the shops – I am normally too busy being stopped by people who want to talk! *TOWIE* has really nice fans, who are always so positive to me. I love chatting with people, whether they watch the show themselves or just want to get pictures for their daughters or whoever. I

There's no question about how well TOWIE has done

never expected it to be this successful – but I am so happy it is! It has been a totally incredible thing to have been part of, and I do still pinch myself sometimes to make sure it's real.

As for our BAFTA win ... wow! We got the YouTube Audience Award at the ceremony in May 2011, and it was just amazing because we were up against these great shows, like *Downton Abbey* and *My Big Fat Gypsy Wedding*.

Amy and I were supposed to be in Marbella, but we changed our flight so we could go to the awards along with the rest of the main cast and the big bosses from Lime Pictures and ITV. We were sat at two tables, and there was such a good vibe. The red carpet was swarming with these amazing celebs – it was overwhelming. By the time it came to our nomination list being read out, we were all so nervous and were holding hands. All the cameras seemed to be on the *My Big Fat Gypsy Wedding* crew, which was a bad sign, but I said I had a feeling it was us.

The Inbetweeners were doing the announcement on stage, and they said the result really quickly, so it took us a few seconds to realise it was us. Then we went mad, and were just jumping up and down and screaming. I was like 'Oh my God, I can't believe it!'

Amy and I were flying to Marbella at 3 a.m. the next morning, so we couldn't stay out and party as much as we wanted to, but we made up for it by going crazy when we got to Marbs!

I sometimes wonder what makes the show so popular, and I think it is because it is so easy to relate to. Most people can relate to at least one of us, and everyone has gone through a lot of the things we go through on the show: relationship and friendship troubles, family issues, gossiping and arguing ... It's what life is made of. But as well as that, it is light-hearted and funny, and there is a spark that you get in people from Essex that can't be copied. I'm not being funny, but have the copycat shows worked as well? No. Because they don't have that spark that we do. I am really proud to be part of TOWIE.

I sometimes wonder what makes the show so popular and I think it is because it is so easy to relate to

The only downside to the show doing so well is that as it has got bigger, so have the egos on it. The vibe used to be one of a group of friends having a laugh, who would hang out together whether the filming was happening or not. Now, at times, people are more engrossed in doing interviews and emailing their agents, or are glaring at each other angrily because of something that was said on camera the week before. It was inevitable that would happen though, I suppose.

One of the biggest egos is Arg. People are surprised by that, but Arg is not as sweet and innocent as he seems – he definitely plays up to his victim role! He and Lauren Goodger are also the worst time-keepers. The two of them are really bad at turning up on time for filming, which gives everyone else the hump. They were

One of the biggest egos is Arg

the worst offenders for this in series three, especially when we filmed the Christmas special, and the bosses were like, 'We're not putting up with this anymore. Anyone who can't be on time from now on is off the show.' Sounds strict, but I reckon it's fair enough – it's really selfish!

The other big ego was, of course, Mark, but you probably guessed that! And somehow he got away with it. He has a very over-powering personality, and he always ends up getting what he wants. Everyone expected me to be really sad to see Mark leave at the end of series three, but I do think it was the right thing for him to do. We discussed it before he made the decision, and he knew it was a big move, but I think it was the right time for him, and he has a great career ahead of him. It's not like I can't see him either, is it? It just means the cameras won't be there, so you lot won't get to see what happens! I think Mark did great in the jungle. He showed people the soft, friendly, loving side of him, which a lot of people don't know, and he did so well to come second. I'm not so sure about his presenting skills on *Take Me Out: The Gossip*, as he seems a bit stiff – he needs to relax more. But I reckon that will come with more experience. He did really well to get it anyhow, so I don't want to knock him for it.

Mark always knew exactly how he wanted to appear on *TOWIE*, and made that happen. I'm not saying that he was always acting exactly, but more that he knew how he wanted to come across and put himself in that mindset before filming started. You can decide for yourself if that means a few acting skills were involved! He didn't care in the beginning how much of a womaniser or lads' lad he came across as – that's how he is, and he was happy for people to know it. But by series three he was doing all the crying and the emotion thing.

Billie and I always say after watching one of those scenes with the boys together, 'And the Oscar for best acting goes to ... Mark and Arg!' Although maybe we're being a bit unfair!

It is one of the questions I get asked most – is it all real? And the answer is exactly what it says on the credits – yes, but some bits are set up for viewers' entertainment.

The people are real, the emotions are real, the relationships are real. It's just that certain situations are set up. And obviously, in order to fill viewers in on what has happened when the cameras have been away, we are often told what to discuss. So if there is a party and the next day someone comes into Minnies when we are being filmed, we are told the conversation should be about the night before.

It is one of the questions I get asked most – is it real? The answer is just as it says on the credits

But what we discuss will have actually happened, and our opinions will be our own.

I really try to be myself on *TOWIE*, and remember who I am, but it is hard because you feel you have to protect yourself and your image a bit and be careful as to how you come across. It's natural that you start worrying what your fans will think, and whether people will judge you. But I think I have done quite a good job of staying true to myself. Looking back at series one, I can see that I have changed, but that is more down to me just growing up. People do mature between the ages of 19 and 21, and it is nice that viewers have been able to see me growing up.

That is one of the reasons why it is good to introduce new

people each series – it gives us old hands a bit of a shake-up, and pulls everyone back to earth. I think they always bring in too many girls though, and not enough boys! I realise the producers are hoping to stir things up, with the girls affecting established relationships and that, but it's about time some nice new men were allowed screen time for us girlies!

The newcomer who shocked me the most when they brought her in was Cara Kilbey in series three. Let's just say I have history with Cara!

On my 17th birthday a group of us, including Billie and Mark's brother Josh, were out at a place called Blake Hall in Ongar. Josh's ex-girlfriend, Brogan, came over and went crazy – I think she was jealous to see him dancing with other girls. She threw drinks over us and was screaming. Billie was upset and went home, but as it was my birthday, I stayed out. About an hour later Cara arrived and started dancing near us. She came over and said she was Brogan's sister – although she isn't – then punched me. We ended up having a bit of a scrap.

I was so upset, and when I got home my mum went mad. Cara is four years older than me, so she should have known better. Six months later she apologised on Facebook, and said that she had been drunk that night. But we hadn't spoken since, so when I heard she was coming on the show, I was like 'Oh my God!' I was actually pretty worried and spoke to the producers, but they had made the decision, and I guess they knew what they were doing. Cara and I eventually talked about what had happened that night, and decided to put it behind us. She seems to have changed, and I am not someone who holds grudges, so we have moved on from it.

The first time we experienced cast members being dropped was at the end of series one – when we were all feeling very comfortable. Candy and Michael, who worked in Sugar Hut, were dropped before the second series, which they weren't happy about, and I am not sure what they are doing now. But that is the way of *TOWIE* – they keep a close eye on who the public are relating to and are interested in, and they are not going to keep filming people that the public don't really connect with. I guess that is what happened with Candy and Michael. It also probably made a difference that whereas the rest of us were good friends before the show, or had links of some kind, none of us really knew Candy and Michael, so there was less of the good interaction.

It was weird when new people were brought into the show in series two. You get kind of protective of it, and feel like they are on your territory. It's like someone new trying to join your group of friends – you need to work them out first!

I remember Amy feeling put out in series two, when she was getting less airtime. I think that because she had a boyfriend who didn't want to appear on *TOWIE*, it made her less interesting for viewers – everyone likes to watch the relationships – but she was not happy when new people on the show, like Joey and Chloe, started getting more onscreen time than her. She thought it was personal, when it wasn't.

I remember Amy feeling put out in series two, when she was getting less airtime

At the same time, I think her management had other ideas

for her and wanted to move her away from *TOWIE*, which is a shame, because I know she really did love her time on the show.

We still tried to keep up our friendship after she left, but the moment I think I realised it really was fading was when I had the launch party for my *Star* magazine column.

I had the party at Zenna Bar in Soho, and I knew a lot of the cast had other things on that night, but I thought the three people closest to me – Billie, Amy and Harry – would all make an effort to be there.

Obviously Billie came, but I thought Harry might not, as it might have been a bit weird for him. He'd had a column in *Star* magazine before me, and then it got dropped and they gave it to me instead, so celebrating my success could understandably have been odd for him. But, bless Harry, he was there, and on great form, chatting and partying, and having a really good time.

No, it was Amy who didn't come, and that made me sad. I know she was nearby that night, but instead of coming to the party just for a bit, she decided to go home. That, to me, was a sign of how things had changed between us.

Amy decided to go home. That, to me, was a sign of how things had changed bewteen us

I can't say for sure whether it was her choice or that of her management, but after she left the show, Amy made a real point of distancing herself from the cast – and that even included me, despite our long friendship, which goes back 15 years. It seemed that what she – or her management – thought would be a good business decision came above our friendship, which is a shame. My priorities will always be my family and friends. I think Amy's are her family and her management. In interviews she has done since, she has said that she has made an effort with me and sent texts, and I don't really know what to make of this, as I don't remember receiving any! I hope she will always be part of my life, but at the moment she is definitely not the person I thought she was.

Another thing a lot of people ask me is how much we get paid for doing the show. The answer for the first series is nothing! Actually no, sorry, we were paid, but it was just £1 each! There is a rule that you can't be under contract without being paid, so we all got that tiny amount. For the second series, the money increased slightly, and we were all paid £50 a day. And then, for series three and four, we were paid weekly, but it was pretty much the same pay. Not exactly a fortune is it?

It is through all the extra stuff that everyone earns their money. We are paid badly on the show – even the producers can't dispute that! – but no one minds, because we earn so much money doing things that are only possible because of the show. Just from photo shoots, interviews and personal appearances, I have made enough in the last year to save for my house and holidays, and live a nice life, so it's been great!

It didn't take long for most people on the show to get managers. You realise quite quickly that you need someone to sort out a lot of stuff for you. From setting up newspaper and magazine interviews and handling any negative press, to dealing with party invites, clothing requests and personal appearances – there is a lot of work going on behind the scenes.

I took on Adam, who works for a company called Money

North. They are the sister company of Girl Management, who I had done my modelling through, so it made sense. Adam really wanted to work with me, which was great, and when we met up he seemed nice and had loads of ideas and plans that made sense to me.

We have a great relationship, and he has become a friend, as well as someone I work with. I think I am the only person on *TOWIE* who has actually stuck with the first manager they got, which I think says something.

I regularly sit down with Adam to discuss what we want to achieve next for me. Between us, we are pretty good at making things happen. At the top of my wish list earlier last year (2011) was that I wanted a column, and I got one soon after with *Star* magazine. I love doing it. It is like keeping a diary that I can look back on one day for the memories, and it is a great way to keep people up to date on my life. I love getting responses to the things I write about, either through *Star* magazine or Twitter. I think I have the best column out of any of the *TOWIE* peeps! Alongside opening Minnies, I think the column has been the other success I am proudest of since the show began.

Also I said last year that I wanted to have a book published – and, well, as you can see, that happened too, and I really hope you have enjoyed it!

For me, all this is just the beginning. I have loads more plans and ideas that I want to make come true. Just wait and see what I have on my wish list for the next year!

DICTIONARY
THE ESSEX LINGO

In Essex there are loads of words that we love using – some
that you'll hear all over the UK, and some that are pretty
unique to us. And if we are ever short of a word or a phrase . . .
well, you can be sure to rely on someone like Joey Essex to
make one up that will take off!

Here are my favourite ones:

Reem – We have Joey to thank for this one! He made it infamous through his 'Look reem, smell reem, be reem'
  catchphrase, but it really just means gorgeous or really cool.
  My favourite way to use it is 'Don't be jel, be reem!' if someone is getting on my nerves.

Shuuttup – The way you should always pronounce 'shut up'.
  But not when you actually want someone to be quiet. Use
  it when you are shocked at what someone is saying. So
  shutting up is actually the last thing you want them to do,
  as they are usually passing on a great piece of gossip!

Glamping – No true Essex girl wants to camp in the traditional way, getting muddy, sleeping on the floor in a

cramped tent and leaving the heels and lashes at home. But glam it up a bit with heeled wellies, designer tents and luxury extras, and suddenly it doesn't seem like such a bad thing after all. It is definitely the only way to camp out at the festivals over the summer!

Vajazzle – Not created by Amy Childs, but definitely made famous by her in the UK. See Chapter 2 for more details on this.

Well jel – Jel is a shortened version of jealous. And if you are very jealous, you are not just jel, you are well jel! A family friend of mine started this, then Billie and I took it up, then Amy picked it up, then before you knew it, it became a *TOWIE* catchphrase.

Marbs – This one is pretty obvious – it's a shortened version of Marbella. Using it probably means you are a regular there.

No Carbs Before Marbs – A saying created by Ellie Redman when she was running a diet class for Arg. It literally means, no carbohydrates before Marbella, but that's not so catchy, is it? It is a motivational saying for when you are getting in shape for your summer holiday.

Definitely – I always put this at the end of sentences when I'm agreeing with someone or emphasising a point. I guess I like to come across as very sure of myself!

ALL MY THANK YOUS!

Oh my God, where do I start! This book has been amazing to put together, but as always, I've had a great team behind me. So these are all people I need to say thanks to ... sorry if I forget anyone, it's not on purpose

Mum, as always you have been an absolute star. You are so strong for me and Billie, and are always there in the background doing everything from making Minnies decisions, to a cup of tea. Thank you for always sticking by me. Love you.

Billie, you are the best sister, and the best friend! I know we will always be there for each other. Team Faiers ☺

Dad, we haven't always had the easiest time of it, but you have always done your best for us and been my true dad. Thank you.

To the rest of my family, Nanny and Grandad, Nanny Wendy, Aunty Libby, Aunty Sam, George, Harvey, Grace, Eva, love you all too!

To my manager and good friend Adam Muddle – you're the best. I couldn't have done this without you. We're a great team, and I know we have a lot more big plans for the future ... so bring it on!

Thanks to the best ghost-writer in showbiz, Emma Donnan, for all your hard work and patience. This book couldn't have been done without you. All those hours in the car on the way to PAs have paid off, not to mention the book bathing sessions on the beach in Dubai!

A big thank you to Carly Cook for believing in this book and being great to work with from moment one. And thanks too to the team at Simon & Schuster, including Emma Harrow, Jo Whitford, Jon Stefani, Dawn Burnett and Lewis Csizmazia.

Thanks to Andrew Lownie for your expertise in the publishing world and for delivering the quickest deal possible in book history!

To my girls Ferne, Charlotte, Molly, Jerri, Kayleigh, Stacey, Gemma, we've had a lot of fun times together – here's to many, many more of them.

Jeff Mehmet – thanks for all your styling and friendship, you have been amazing, and Johanna Dalemo, you make my hair and make-up just perfect! Claire Tipler, you are the most loyal nail technician ever, and give me amazing toes and fingers – thanks!

To my Minnies girls, Sue, Lyn, Nicola, Davina, Chloe, Alison and Charlotte, the shop wouldn't be what it is without you, so thanks for all your hard work. And Mum and Libby, your seven-day weeks are incredible. You're all great.

Thanks to the rest of Money & Money North – Martin and Kate O'Shea, Emma Rouse, Francis Ridley, Dana Malstrom, Sophie Luard, Jack Aylott, Joe Foster and Paula Stewart.

Thanks also to Andy and Leon at Industry Music Group for all your hard work, and Ian and Dave at Peace of Mind Ltd – I know I can rely on you to always have my back! Adam Sutherland and Trevor Adams at Matrix, Robin Kennedy at Cruise Pictures – you are snappers extraordinaire!

All the magazines and newspapers that have supported me, especially the team at *Star* magazine, I have really appreciated it.

Gary Smith and Ben Webster at ITV Press Office, and Mark Boustead, you have all been a great part of the *TOWIE* press family.

And of course thanks to the team on *TOWIE* and at Lime Pictures – you gave me my break, and I won't forget it!